Casting Lots

Casting Lots

Creating a Family in a Beautiful, Broken World

Susan Silverman

DA CAPO PRESS
A Member of the Perseus Books Group

Designed by Cynthia Young
Set in 11 point Adobe Caslon Pro

Library of Congress Cataloging-in-Publication Data
Names: Silverman, Susan, author.
Title: Casting lots : creating a family in a beautiful, broken world /
Susan   Silverman.
Description: Boston, MA : Da Capo Press, 2015.
Identifiers: LCCN 2015027877| ISBN 9780306824616 (hardcover) |
ISBN 9780306824623 (e-book)
Subjects: LCSH: Silverman, Susan. | Jewish women—United States—Biography.
Classification: LCC E184.37.S56 A3 2015 | DDC 305.48/8924073—dc23 LC record
available at http://lccn.loc.gov/2015027877

First Da Capo Press edition 2016
Published by Da Capo Press
A Member of the Perseus Books Group
www.dacapopress.com

Da Capo Press books are available at special discounts for bulk purchases in the U.S. by corporations, institutions, and other organizations. For more information, please contact the Special Markets Department at the Perseus Books Group, 2300 Chestnut Street, Suite 200, Philadelphia, PA, 19103, or call (800) 810-4145, ext. 5000, or e-mail special.markets@perseusbooks.com.

10 9 8 7 6 5 4 3 2 1

For Aliza Rose, Hallel Ma'ayan,
Adar Daniel, Zamir Gidon, and Ashira Eliraz.

I love you the whole earth and the whole sky.

Contents

Part 3

Prologue

My whole life I felt like God's bitch. Begging, negotiating, bargaining for the safety of my loved ones—particularly my mother. I offered random promises—what else did I have to give? Cut my long braids? Sacrifice Karen Marie, the doll I shared my bed with despite her large, hard plastic shape lest she feel unloved? Shun *The Brady Bunch* and *The Partridge Family* on Friday nights?—like how I'd be vigilant, agree to watch over them, never leave under my own steam for parties or school, and never ever allow myself to get dragooned into a sleepaway camp. I'd hold my breath a full minute. Or at recess I'd purposely get an out in kickball in exchange for my parents still being alive when the 3 p.m. bell rang and the school day was over.

It seemed to work. My parents were alive (although dead they may have had a happier marriage). But it was little use trying to banish the fears: vivid images of car crashes and burglaries that awaited my family in my absence. *It's possible Mom is dead right now.* The principal's secretary brings a note for my teacher. I analyze her face. Is she stealing a glance at me? Is that smile a ruse—hiding the news she bears? I have already figured out that the police who were called to the scene of my mother's death had

determined? that her daughter—the poor child still innocently un-
aware of the tragedy that has befallen her—was sitting in the third
row, second seat back at Webster School on Elm Street, and soon
I would be across from Principal McMahan at his big desk and he
would be looking at his hands, afraid to tell me. Is that faraway
sound a siren? The light in the distance an ambulance? I should
never have left! *Okay God, if I run nonstop until I get home will you
keep them safe?*

I never stepped on a crack while on my way to the local market,
clutching dimes for Sky Bars, Reese's Cups and Mallomars. I sus-
pected that where I stepped had no impact on my mother's fate,
but I couldn't chance it. Constantly fighting any separation from
my mother was a kind of exile—an estrangement of my mind that
yearned for rationality from my heart that knew the world was irrational and that at any second the Big Guy could flick me a booger
and whomp, my mother would be gone. I had to keep Him con-
scious—and protective—of us. I had to lobby him. I had to keep
Him happy.

By the fourth grade, completing the five-minute walk to school
in our quiet, suburb-like North Manchester neighborhood was
nearly impossible. "Will you be home when I get back?" I called
out repeatedly to my mother as I inched down the cement
walkway.

"Yes," she said with a wave of the hand that was less a "bye-bye"
and more of a fingers-flicking "shoo" motion.

"Promise?"

"I promise."

"Swear?"

"I swear."

"But, Mom, how can you be *sure* nothing will happen to you?"

I must have been impossible to raise. If I were my mother I'd be negotiating with God for me *not* to come home.

My six-year-old sister Laura would watch me with her bright-green almond eyes, waiting for my every hesitant step, and decide I was hopeless. She'd head to her first-grade class on her own, her golden curls bobbing, while I doubled back, creeping around the side of the house and pressing my nose to the sliding-glass door, hands cupped around my eyes, peering in at my mother as she made apple slices for Sarah, who smiled happily in her high chair. Oh, to sit and watch *Mr. Rogers' Neighborhood* and *Captain Kangaroo* with Sarah, eating crackers and cheese my mom would arrange in a wooden bowl laced with an open napkin!

My mother would notice me and unlock the door. Now the world felt right. God was back in His cage, and I could relax.

My mother looked like Marlo Thomas in *That Girl*. When she wore her flared brown pants with patterns of giant orange and white leaves, a pale silk top, big silver hoop earrings, and an expertly attached fall with a flip at the ends, she confirmed my overall sense that I was living in the same house with a famous actress. I knew I would stay up half the night to make sure she and my father came home safely from their night out, that there had been no fire in the movie theater or smashup on the road home. I'd distract myself watching *Wolfman Jack* and *Vampira* and, if I was lucky, a late-night appearance of *Green Acres* or *Family Affair*—hoping my parents would return before "The Star-Spangled Banner" introduced static and I would be left utterly alone.

The shape of my life formed itself around ragged fears of death. It demanded vigilance. "Honey, everything is fine," my mother whispered as she tried to lull me to sleep. "Just lie down and think sweet thoughts."

I knew better. Inattention for even a moment had dire consequences. God knows, it had happened before.

If Zoloft had existed when I was in college, would I still have married Yosef? From the start I nestled, trembling, into his sense of well-being, embracing his religious practice, activism and purposefulness. With him, my sense of death lurking everywhere subsided to an underground rattle, an earthquake that *probably* would not erupt, although my fear-mongering imagination still offered up such classics as Yosef and our six- and four-year-old daughters Flattened on the Highway in our Ford Taurus by a Tractor-Trailer Slipping out of Control.

Yet, here I was, six thousand miles from them and from our home in Boston, about to add another family member to my *Oh God please don't let them die* list. In defiance of the horrors that I feared awaited everyone I loved, today I would meet my new son.

It was Sunday, October 9, 1999, and the rains were falling hard, even though it was a month past the Ethiopian winter. The East African skies opened on my sister Jody and me, flooding the courtyard as our driver pulled up outside a two-story gray building: the African Cradle Children's Center, my muddy, run-down Promised Land. Children who had been tossing around a broken plastic car ran to us, smiling, waving, calling *Missus, Missus,* joining in the ambient chorus of splashing, honking, and squeaky metal. Rivulets of water flowed comfortingly through the dirt, splashing muddy toes that poked through shoes whose tips had been cut off to make room for growing feet. *Missus, Missus.*

The rain somehow made the moment right for me. Throughout the winters of my childhood, cold, wet weather kept my family indoors, safe and together, and now this drenching rain would keep my son and me cozy on our first morning together.

He was just behind this door—among all the other orphaned babies, lying lined up in their cribs, the older ones standing and grasping the bars, bah-bah-ing for attention, raising their arms to passing caregivers. This, for me, was not only a Promised Land—the gift of my new son—but also a kind of ground zero, a real-life incarnation of my lifelong fears: children who had lost everyone. I wanted to save them all. Adopt each and every one of them. Yosef and I could add more beds to the kids' rooms, establish one of those big-family routines, pile into the mini-bus each morning on our way to the Jewish Day School. I'd adopt all the older kids clamoring behind us in the yard, too. And what of the ones Jody and I had passed in the street on the way here, smiling, their hands outstretched? The magnitude was dizzying and diminishing. *Please God, give them all loving families!*

I tried to temper my fears. Focus on the moment. *Right now, all that matters is my son and me.* I would put on emotional blinders to guard against the pull of all the other deserving children in the world who also needed mommies and daddies. As I lifted my hand in a gentle fist to knock on the orphanage door, I resolved to allow just one little boy on the other side to become, at least for the moment, my whole world.

The door opened before I even had a chance to knock.

Part 1

Chapter 1

Adar Hill

*L*ike his sisters, Aliza Rose and Hallel Ma'ayan, Adar Daniel Abramowitz-Silverman would have more syllables in his name than John Jacob Jingleheimer Schmidt. Names I wrapped around them like protective armor. He began transforming our lives from the moment we saw the first pictures of him.

At first, we knew him only as Daniel, the "paperwork name" they gave him when he arrived at the orphanage in Addis Ababa. We decided to call him Adar, a Hebrew name drawn from the Jewish calendar month in which our paperwork and his were stapled together. We held out this name for him, open and waiting like a warm fluffy towel at the seaside for a child running cold and blue-lipped from the waves.

Waiting for a glimpse of his face was torture. His picture was never on the adoption website because our match was made before his profile had been uploaded. It was eleven days and thirteen hours before the thick manila envelope arrived. It finally appeared in the mailbox the third time I checked that day, the fifty-fourth time since I had perfected the ritual of slowly opening the mailbox while saying "please-please-please." The sun was high in a pale blue sky and a chill hovered over our covered porch, but that's not why I shivered as I stared at the return address label: *African Cradle Children's Center.* I solemnly took the envelope to the dining room table and took a deep breath. It was the last moment of not knowing the face of my child.

The photos that spilled out on the table showed a round face with wide, focused eyes, and full red lips that my sister Laura would later describe as "little silk pillows." He was lying on a baby bouncer, his head and upper body raised. He wore white one-piece pajamas with the outlines of butterflies, over which was a blue and white bib shaped like a dog's face. His tiny bare feet poked out at the ends, their softness visible.

He was beautiful.

I savored each shot of my son like the first sip of coffee in the morning. "Aliza, Hallel *and Adar,*" I said, melding our children into one family.

"Wow. Wow, wow, wow," was Yosef's reaction when I brought the photos to his office. His small nonprofit of Jewish educational websites had grown to a staff of twelve, each of whom was equally excited for news from Ethiopia. Yosef held up one picture where Adar's mouth made an O shape, eyes wide in amusement.

"I *know,*" I said, beaming. "It's like he's saying, 'I am no mere subject for your camera. *I* am also looking at *you.*'"

We had waited until we had the physical proof to tell Aliza, five, and Hallel, three, about their new brother. I was itching for the evening ahead, our big plan for breaking the news to them: hiking to a beautiful setting, showing them the pictures and relishing their excitement. I hoped Yosef remembered to bring the video camera. What a moment it would be!

Late that afternoon, the girls and I met Yosef at Cold Spring Park. We would now and forever know this place as Adar Hill. "It was where I first saw your face and knew that my life was complete," I imagined Aliza saying to a standing-room-only crowd at her brother's future bar mitzvah. I could easily see that day: Aliza would be eighteen then, poised and articulate. Her hair would be brushed. Hallel would be sixteen, her eyes finally in sync with each other—not, as my sister Laura described, "so crossed it's like they're trying to switch sockets." She will honor her Ethiopian brother's Jewish rite of passage in a watercolor she had painted of Adar Hill.

Yosef and I did good ritual, and this plan was perfect. I was an ordained rabbi, and together we had written a Jewish parenting book. We had this stuff *down*. We would go up Adar Hill, where each of us in turn would offer the baby a blessing. I could already hear Aliza and Hallel's little voices in my head: *May you get lots of kisses in Ethiopia. May you come home soon. May you have sweet dreams.* "Girls, stop kissing the pictures so much!" I'd have to mock-scold them. Then we'd sing *shehecheyanu,* a blessing that thanks God for bringing us to a special moment. The girls would dance to our happy song.

The four of us ambled toward one of the small hills just off the trail. Dry and crusty leaves, liberated from months under ice and snow, crunched beneath our feet. Tiny green promises of spring on the tips of the tree branches broke through the barrenness. I patted my jacket pocket for the photos like a traveler feeling for her passport.

It was chilly but dry, and we were bundled in heavy sweaters. "It's cold," Aliza complained.

"Why are we here?" Hallel asked with an edge of complaint.

"You'll see, sweetie," I said in a perfect singsong, hoping my coyness wouldn't send her into a fit of Hallel-rage that would surely spoil the plan. Instead of the perfect ritual, Yosef would carry a kicking child to the van, Aliza would be relieved and I would be furious at everyone.

But fortunately, we quietly continued on. Our silent ascent, with only the sounds of our footsteps and the occasional snapping twig, made me think of our biblical father, Abraham, walking up a different mountain with his son, Isaac, on his way to heed God's call to sacrifice the boy. Their walk was defined by a silence interrupted by only a single interaction. "Father," Isaac said. "Here is the wood, but where is the sheep for the burnt offering?" Abraham answered, "God will provide the offering, my son."

What kind of God would call parents to sacrifice their son? A distant, impervious, indifferent God. The same God, I imagined, that in stark silence had demanded as much from Adar's birth mother, whose fate the adoption agency hadn't known. The same God that had randomly granted us her child.

Abraham bound Isaac to an altar and held the knife in the air above him. An angel of God called out, "Abraham! Abraham! Do not raise your hand against the boy!" Abraham looked up and saw a ram caught in the brambles—the true sacrifice. Suddenly God was no longer an indifferent absence. God was the ability to stretch and transform reality—to save a child. This was an ability life's circumstances had granted me, but had not granted my new son's birth mother.

Upon our own little mountain, Aliza sat on Yosef's lap, protected from the cold ground, and Hallel sat on mine, wiggling her tush to get comfortable. I breathed in Hallel's hair and kissed her head, so grateful that I could hold my daughters, raise them, love them. That I would also be the mother of this new baby boy. Joggers and dog-walkers passed below us. *Hey, down there, want to see some pictures?*

"Girls, we have a surprise for you," I said. "You have a new baby brother!"

"His name is Adar, and he's a month old," Yosef added.

I looked at the girls expectantly, smiling broadly to encourage the same from them.

Hallel spoke first. "Can we get pizza?" she said.

"Pizza!" agreed Aliza, jumping up. They both began running down the hill, bound for pizza.

"Wait!" I called. "We have pictures!" I waved them in the air like an evangelist with a pamphlet.

Our perfect moment had sucked. Yosef put his arm around me. "I'm sorry, honey. I know it didn't go as you hoped," he said.

"Self-centered little shits," I said about my five- and three-year-olds.

That night, the wind whistling softly through the open window, tinkling the wooden box of chimes I had placed on the windowsill when we moved in, imagining the peaceful, quaint childhood the room would hold, Hallel cried out in her sleep. She tossed and turned, her face scrunched. A tear ran down one cheek.

"Mama's here, sweetie girl, everything's okay," I whispered. *Oh God, did something horrible happen to her?* I scanned my mind for any unsavory staff working at her day care. Or maybe she was longing for, worried for, her baby brother?

"No, stop. Stop it!" she said.

"What's the matter, baby?" I spoke gently, stroking her head.

More weepy tossing. *Tell me, baby! What is it?*

Finally she called out, loudly and clearly, "Stop copying me!"

Hallel did not take kindly to imitation. That would be her nightmare, even at age three, that others were copying her thoughtful, intricate drawings and paintings. No, she was not reliving a secret trauma, or longing for Adar. I laughed. This sweet combination of surprise and familiarity deepened my tenderness toward her. As I kissed her forehead, I thought of my son, still a mystery, a continent away, far beyond my touch. I wondered if he awoke crying in the night. If his birth mother, if she were still alive, reached for him in her dreams.

By morning the girls seemed to have acclimated to the news and were even excited. They huddled over Adar's pictures, laying them out on the table in order of their favorites, negotiating the relative merits of each. "He has big eyes," Hallel said, comically widening her narrow green ones. "I think he's talking here," Aliza said, making her lips round like his and saying, "Oooohhh."

Soon they were dancing around the table, scream-singing his name and waving the photos like flags. It was *Lord of the Flies* meets Barney. They pulled a picture of the two sisters off the refrigerator and placed their favorite Adar pic next to it. I was dispatched to our home office to make copies of the combined photos so they could show their friends and teachers the three siblings together. They had a brother!

On our way to New Hampshire to show my parents their new grandson, I ignored the exact change in the ashtray and chose a lane with a tollbooth attendant.

"Really, honey?" Yosef said as I reached into my pocketbook and pulled out a dollar and the pictures.

At my mom's house, my four parents gathered to "meet" Adar—my dad and his wife, Janice; and my mom and her husband, John. My family doesn't make distinctions among "step," "half," or, to some extent, "ex." "Adopted" was certainly not going to be a defining category.

We met at Mom's, where I made John a cup of coffee. I took pride in it because I was the only person who made the coffee strong enough for his taste. Also, he was so self-sufficient and quietly, constantly helpful to us all that it brought me joy to do anything, even something small, for him. One fall Sunday as he was sweeping my back porch, I said, "John, why do you help us so much?" He paused, held the broom steady, and said, "Because it makes my life better." I knew that this new baby grandson would make his life even better.

What a motley crew it was around the large, round kitchen table: my mother in her jeans and flannel button-down; John in his beige khakis and light-blue work shirt; Janice in her workout clothes, her white sneakers stark against her somehow still tanned legs, wearing the diamond ring her first husband gave her ("It's a perfectly good ring, just 'cuz he was a schmuck"); and my dad in the official red Target employee shirt emblazoned with a white circle near the left shoulder that he managed to get through the employees' website after Janice suggested he add some designer labels to his wardrobe, "for when we're in Boca." "Hey, this shirt has a label," he had argued.

"It's amazing," my father said in his thick New Hampshire accent as he gazed at the pictures. "He's a random kid on the other side of the world, and I love him already. I'd do anything for him. How can that be? It's un-fuckin' believable."

"Oy, oy, oy, Susie! Is he eva gaw-jess!" said Janice. "He's gonna be a real lady killa."

"He's mighty fine," said John, always dignified and able to convey deep love with sparse words. Whenever I say, "I love you, John," he replies, "And I you, my dear," but it carries just as much oomph as my dad's "Oy! Love ya to pieces, honey!"

An orphanage in eastern Africa immediately became an outpost of our home, a satellite location of our daily lives, as if Ethiopia were Adar's bedroom, right next to the girls' room. Talking about Adar, guessing what he might be like, choosing blankets and sheets for him, imagining his—and therefore our—mythical ancestors, made Adar grow in our hearts from March to October, when I would travel to Addis Ababa and bring our son home.

The pictures thrust my mother into high gear. She began making a list of things to send Adar—vitamins, a mobile for his crib to increase his IQ, family pictures, clothing. Her grandson was going to have the best start in life he could; she would see to that. And maybe our busy, far-away tending would keep him safe.

Chapter 2

Maybe Just the Cruise

J was not yet a year old when my mother became a contestant on her favorite TV game show, *Concentration*. It was a rebus puzzle in which players paired numbered squares on a giant grid, hoping to find a match and win prizes. When they got a match, the two squares pivoted to reveal more clues to the puzzle.

Beth Ann, my beautiful, restless mother, had wandered over to where they taped the show at Rockefeller Center when she and Donald were with his parents, Rose and Max, on their annual trip to Manhattan to buy the fall line of boys' clothes and scout uniforms for Max's store, The Varsity Shop, on Main Street in Concord, New Hampshire. She had so recently been a French and theater major at Tufts University—and now, her life as a mother and retail wife left her at a loss intellectually.

Enjoying the high beams of the studio lights, green-eyed, fresh-faced Beth Ann Silverman continued to make matches, suss out the puzzle and answer questions. The twenty-two-year-old from Manchester, New Hampshire, had already won ten consecutive games. "Truth is stranger than fiction?" she guessed, piecing together the exposed parts of a tooth, a muscled arm, a cartoon man holding a wrench and a hand in a "stop" position.

With that, Beth Ann was on her way to the Tournament of Champions.

The show's host tried to stump this girl-on-a-roll with an extra question. "SCUBA is an acronym for *what phrase?*" asked Hugh Downs, drawing it out for drama.

Beth Ann surprised even herself as the correct answer flew from her lips. "Self-Contained Underwater Breathing Apparatus?"

Applause.

"Ed, tell us what Mrs. Silverman has won so far!" said Hugh Downs sounding, to her ear, disappointed that she knew the answer. Announcer Ed McMahon's familiar, resonant voice rang out, and intensified as the list went on: *A Triumph Spitfire sports car! A twenty-four-foot speedboat! A twenty-seven-foot party barge! This living room set!* Ed sounded as if he might explode when he reached the crescendo: *AND A SEVEN-NIGHT, EIGHT-DAY LUXURY CRUISE TO BERMUDA!*

That night in their hotel room, Donald Silverman hoisted his wife and spun her around. I picture her catching their fleeting reflections in the large hotel window, her head back, wavy brown hair lifting free behind her. Donald and Beth Ann: winners, partners, lovers, and now with oodles of stuff—boats, furs, luggage, clothes, a sports car.

Later, after the giddiness was gone, they lay on the hotel-room bed. "We'll have to sell it all, you know," said Donald. "We need the cash."

"But . . . "

"Hey, I'm the shmuck who pays the bills."

Donald's father had never once spoken a kind word to his boy, whose only relief from his father's meanness had been summers at Camp Samoset, his most treasured memory. But now he had put aside his master's degree in social work and his lifelong dream to build a boys' camp for at-risk kids, and spent six days a week sorting and selling clothing at his father's store. It was a small but necessary income to support himself and his bride, a woman he had initially recklessly adored, and who now grated on his nerves.

Beth Ann lay in the dark, deflated. It seemed like it was always this way with Donald. Two years earlier, she had tried to break off their engagement after driving to New York to see *Guys and Dolls* on Broadway. She came out of the show feeling lighter than she had in weeks, singing and skipping along the sidewalk, serenading passers-by: *Luck be a lady tonight!*

"Beth Ann, stop it," Donald said. "You're acting like a fucking crazy person."

He ran ahead to the car to smoke cigarettes. Way behind him, Beth Ann made a left instead of a right and didn't catch up for another half hour, by which time she was crying. She called off the wedding, but Donald managed to woo her back by being funny and self-deprecating again, just like on their first date when he showed up in a suit and tie at the insistence of his landlady—a friend of Beth Ann's parents, Goldie and Herman. When Beth Ann, an artsy Tufts student who was casually dressed with a bandana in her hair, opened the door to see Donald's skinny frame in his best suit, they both laughed.

Falling back into Donald's charms was easier for Beth Ann than facing her mother, who had commandeered the wedding preparations like a zealot preparing for the Messiah. Only years later did she understand her mother's fervor in light of how Goldie's own first engagement, at age eighteen, was called off by the boy's parents when they saw the back-road hovel she and her family lived in.

On September 3, 1961, Beth Ann and Donald walked bravely, stoically down the aisle into this life together.

Now, outside their hotel-room window, the city's neon flashed like ambulance lights. It wasn't that Beth Ann wanted or needed all those prizes—certainly not the furs or fancy car—but she would have liked to bask in her moment a little longer.

"Donnie, couldn't we keep just some of it?" she asked as her moment of glory faded. "I went twenty-seven rounds; even Hugh Downs said it was a record."

Donald sighed as he snapped off the bedside light. "Maybe just the cruise."

Nine months later, my brother, Jeffrey Michael, was born. Three months after that was the expiration date for the cruise, so my parents had to take it. Beth Ann thought that getting away might help the marriage. Donald was desperate for a break from working for his father.

Both sets of grandparents were delighted to have a baby apiece to dote on. My mother's parents in Waterbury, Connecticut, would take care of me for a week. Max and Rose in Concord, New Hampshire, a few towns away, took the baby. My parents set off on the cruise from New York, and over the seven days of bright sun reflecting off the ocean Donald turned a deep brown, while Beth Ann grew pink and tender to the touch—even though she spent most of her time painting the view from the shaded balcony of their cabin. "Jesus, Beth Ann," Donald complained. "At least take a swim."

At the end of the cruise, they were going to take a few days to visit the 1964 World's Fair, whose theme was "Peace Through Understanding." They arrived mid-morning on a Friday at their hotel in Queens, still dressed in their disembarkation best—Donald in a suit and Beth Ann in Rose's three-piece double-knit. They were sweaty and uncomfortable, and dying for the cool relief of the hotel shower. As they checked in, some excited fans mistook Donald for Sandy Koufax, the left-handed Jewish pitcher for the Dodgers. He happily obliged them, standing for pictures and signing autographs. *To Marjorie, Keep swinging! SK. To Gerry, Run on home! Sandy.* Nobody seemed to notice that he signed with his right hand.

In the room, they dropped their suitcases, and my mother stood inside the door with her hands over her face in gleeful embarrassment. My father watched her with a grin.

Before starting their day strolling the grounds of the fair, they decided to call their parents to check on the kids. The black curly phone wire stretched and retreated, stretched and retreated with my father's characteristic pacing, his nerves already on edge at the thought of speaking to his father again. But it was his father's best friend, Fred Berman, who answered the phone.

"Donny," Fred said. "We have bad news. Jeffrey's gone."

"What do you mean, gone?" Donald's first thought was that his son had been kidnapped, like the Lindbergh baby.

"I'm so sorry, Donny. There was nothing we could do."

My parents rushed home in a daze. Donald's brother, Lewis, and Beth Ann's sister, Martha, who were briefly dating at the time, picked them up at the airport in Boston for the hour-and-a-half drive north to Rose and Max's house. When my parents saw me sitting at a round table in the corner of the room—dazed, wide-eyed and pale—they rushed over and held me in a little closed huddle, just the three of us.

In the fading New Hampshire evening light, it took Donald and Beth Ann a few moments to locate the normally garrulous

Nana and Papa, who now sat shrunken among their friends on the turquoise, L-shaped couch. Turquoise, like the endless sparkling sea that surrounded them. Was that only yesterday?

Rose, who was usually poised, coiffed and well dressed, was still in her bathrobe and slippers.

"How can you ever forgive me?" Max cried, looking up at his son. The normally debonair man now with swollen eyes and a five o'clock shadow, his bare white ankles protruding above his brown leather house shoes. This man who had loomed so large and terrifying over his son now appeared so small. Donald, still holding me in his arms, was stunned—even strangely thrilled—by the power he suddenly felt over his father.

It seems that Jeffrey had still been quiet in his crib at 8 a.m., so Rose had taken the opportunity to have a piece of burnt toast with margarine and black coffee, her regular breakfast. Max had gone into the guest room to check on the baby.

"Rose, where's Jeffrey?" he yelled.

Rose rushed to the bedroom. The wire frame holding the mattress had slipped from a corner hook, and the mattress had slanted down. Jeffrey's head had been wedged into the corner between the wooden frame and the mattress, his small body concealed by the crumpled blanket.

They lifted him out. His face was blue. They called their neighbor, a doctor, who had run across the street and up the long path of the steep, stone steps that led to the front door.

Beth Ann knelt before her mother-in-law, held her hand, and moved a clump of stiffly frosted hair from Rose's eyes. She knew she couldn't cry. That would destroy her in-laws. *Mom, it was an accident. It's not your fault. These things just happen sometimes.*

"Your friends took care of the house for you," Rose said quietly.

My mother let the strange comment pass and busied herself making coffee and serving cake to the guests who offered reassurances. *You'll have more children. This one's gone, but God will give you another. The important thing is to forget this ever happened.*

That night, in their small duplex apartment, alone with their grief, Donald and Beth Ann walked hand in hand to Jeffrey's room to smell his baby clothes, touch his crib, hold his soft coverlet. They opened the door and found it entirely empty, except for the white rocking chair with the flowers and vines my mother had painted, and a small pile of sawdust where the crib's hinges had been unscrewed.

Chapter 3

I Got Love

The rabbi gave my parents a small cardboard box that reminded them of the pale brown pinewood coffin that had been lowered into the ground that day. It was decorated with images of Jerusalem, and inside was a memorial candle that would burn for seven days, plus a photocopied page with a transliterated Mourner's Kaddish, a prayer extolling God's magnificence, traditionally spoken by the bereaved. On another piece of paper were a few psalms in English and Hebrew. My father pulled matches from the thin clear lining of his pack of cigarettes.

Donald and Beth Ann groped for solace through Jewish ritual even though it seemed irrelevant—bygone relics clutched by older, European immigrants. "May you be comforted among the mourners of Zion," the rabbi said in his Polish accent. My parents didn't know how to respond. Was "thank you" the right thing to say? Were they really among the mourners of Zion? In their grief, they didn't feel part of anything, all alone in their late-night kitchen as they watched the flickering flame struggle to catch enough wick to grow.

"Donny," my mother said when they huddled in bed that night. "Don't shut off the light yet."

My father read to her from a book of Sholem Aleichem short stories, and that became their ritual for months—he reading aloud, she with her head on his chest before drifting off to sleep. There was no meaning in God or candles or Zion, but there was meaning in stories. It was to be the most loving and tender time of their marriage, as if God had taken Jeffrey and, in return, gave them tenderness. As if the vacation Beth Ann had hoped would bring them together had worked its magic after all.

Donald went back to the store that spring just as the camping stock arrived in large cartons—scout uniforms, tents, flashlights, all the mundane tasks of retail. But working for Max was different now. It was like going home to find that Daredevil Hill was no more than a slope in the road. "This is what I want or I quit," Donald said to his chastened father. From then on, Donald charted his path to owning and expanding the business. He also turned his work into an outlet for his social-worker inclinations: hiring kids from the foster care system whom he could also mentor, encourage, and clothe for free. He changed Max's hard and fast rule that the customer is always right. If a parent hit or belittled a child in Donald's presence, they were told, quite bluntly, to leave. He put anti-war and anti-racism posters on the walls. If customers didn't like his politics, they could fuck themselves—and then shop elsewhere.

For my mother, it was different. She faced wide-open, empty days and the tormenting thoughts of "if only." She found a bit of solace by pushing me in the stroller along the sidewalks of Manchester. Outside the house was a sense of forward movement, of possibility. She returned to the weekly bridge club at her friend

Margie's, trying to laugh and chat with the few other Jewish women in Manchester. She looked out the bay window to the fall foliage, the vibrancy capturing her artist's eye, and she mixed paint colors in her mind.

Margie had just set down a fresh cup of black coffee. I reached up to grab it. Whoosh! The boiling liquid burned through my skin. My mother, instinctively spurning the frantic advice of her friends to spread Vaseline on the burn, rushed me to the sink and ran cold water over the raw flesh. Carrying me out the door, a clean dish-towel wrapped around my skinless arm, she told Margie to call the pediatrician to say she was on her way and then to call Donald and let him know.

I didn't stop screaming as I lay on the back seat of the car. My father, by his account, sobbed as hard as I did as he drove the half hour from his job after yet another bad-news phone call regarding one of his children. *I'll do anything*, he pleaded aloud, despite his devout atheism. *I'll work for my father forever. I'll never leave Beth Ann. Just let Susie be okay.*

With my arm wrapped in white bandages, I slept that night and through most of the next day. My mother spent the time disinfecting my room. She buffed the rungs of my crib, scrubbed the walls, scoured the baseboards and polished the floor, even cleaning the corners with a toothbrush. The whole room smelled like Pine-Sol. Cleanliness would keep the germs away, protect her baby from the harm that the universe could (and did) deliver at any moment.

After that I cried at bedtime every night. I fought sleep. Even when I succumbed, sleep wouldn't hold me. Glassy-eyed, I'd wander out, sobbing, to my exhausted and at-wits'-end parents. The first time they tried to leave me with a babysitter for an evening out, I called every survival instinct into play. I knew at the deepest level that the world was divided between home and abyss.

A year passed, and in it my mother's belly had swelled again. This time a baby girl was born. Laura slept deeply, ate happily, and watched the world through her piercing green eyes—almost adult-like. When she was six months old, our mother taped a little pink bow to Laura's exceptionally bald head to identify her as a girl, but soon enough she grew thick golden curls. She was exquisite. As we grew, her calm, her seeming sense that all was right with the world, was an increasing fascination to me.

"I was meant to be the daddy of girls!" our father would come to say, like a mantra, arms widespread. "I guess that's what God wanted for me."

God? Strange, because my father's atheism was a point of pride.

My parents built a perfect, self-enclosed world—a four-bed-room ranch house, under the strict direction of my mother's father, Herman, who owned a lumberyard. Nothing about this house was out of place. A stocked pantry off the kitchen, a fireplace in the living room, a light-blue bathtub with baby shampoo and Dove soap nestled on the corner ledge.

By the time I was six and Laura was three, we had small rituals. Family dinners. We listened to Broadway musical albums nights and weekends. Every few weeks after our nightly bath, we'd sit on the cool countertop in our pajamas, towels draped over our shoulders. Our mother pulled the long, narrow hair scissors from the bathroom drawer, and I felt the tickle of the sharp silver point against the back of my neck, my forehead, and around my ears, and then my mother's cool breath blowing away the snippets: "A pixie cut for my pixie." Laura's hair was shoulder length, and she'd have a trim. Our father might peek in and say, "Watcha doin'?" To which Laura and I would respond, "Getting a haircut." That was the opening for him to respond, "Why don't ya get 'em all cut!" But it could go the other way, too. "Jesus, Beth Ann," he might say. "It's almost 9. Some of us have to work tomorrow." When he was his sweet funny self, I believed he would never be sarcastic again. When he was mad, it was impossible to imagine him ever *not* mad.

I dreaded my father's insistence on bedtime. Most nights, unable to close my eyes, I left my room, wondrous at Laura's sound sleep, to slip my long skinny self between my parents—each turned away to their edge of the bed. In their marriage, my mother had retreated into chores, art, and her television programs. My father, into music and books. I teetered in the bed between them—deliberately, cautiously erring toward my mother before lying down. Only there, beside her, could I sleep soundly.

Once in a great while a Jewish ritual found its way into our kitchen. *Fiddler on the Roof* was one of the musicals that filled our house, and our father would hold us on his lap and sing "Far From the Home I Love." He had a terrible singing voice, but he conveyed such sweetness and pain in that song when he sang it that it was beautiful. I imagined Anatevka on the rare Friday nights when Mom pulled two heavy gold candlesticks down from the high cupboard. "Grandma's mother, Ida Trapsky, carried them from Poland on a boat across the Atlantic," she told us. Did Great-Grandma Ida walk, like Tevye and Golda, in a ragged parade of families and wagons toward an unknown world? I tried to summon an image of her as a young woman, two small daughters at her side, her belongings wrapped to her body with cloth. I touched the cool metal of the candlesticks and slid them slowly across the Formica countertop to feel the fear and hope in their weight. Maybe she needed God with her on her journey. Maybe God needed her to make that journey.

We leaned on the kitchen counter, silently watching the match come to life, smelling the sulfur. Unfolded paper napkins fluttered atop our hair at our mother's request. "You're supposed to wear a head covering," she explained before she sang the blessings she proudly remembered from third-grade Hebrew school. In our warm, darkened kitchen, the combination of flames and the secret language we chanted by rote exposed something hidden. Was that thing God?

One fall day, as first grade began, our mother sat Laura and me down on her bed, our feet hanging off the edge. "Daddy is going to live next door with the Coopers for a while," she said.

Laura cried. I was dumbfounded.

Our father called on the phone from work, right on cue, and I begged him to come home. "I'll be right next door. You can see me whenever you want," he said, sobbing. "I love you so much, my baby."

A month later, my father came to stay with us while my mother went to visit her sister in Maryland. The first morning, I climbed onto the yellow stool by the small stationery counter in the kitchen, under the phone, where my mother kept pens, paper, and hair supplies. It's where she brushed and plaited my hair into two smooth, perfectly even braids before school each morning. My father attempted a few strokes with the brush and then tried to divide my hair, twisting and untwisting it, until he dissolved into tears.

"It's okay, Daddy," I said. "I'll wear it down today."

When my mother returned from her trip, my father stayed. "We can't live without each other," they said, and I repeated that mantra to myself for years afterward, even as they continued down their hopeless and increasingly desperate attempts to buttress their marriage.

Laura and I became soft, tentative bridges between parents who were rarely in the same room together. Our father spent weekend mornings in the living room, where he read and listened to music,

Laura often curled on his lap, with Kurt Vonnegut, John Irving, Elie Wiesel, Philip Roth and J. D. Salinger open in his hands. I sang to the Broadway album on the record player, sometimes following the words on the stiff cover with my long, skinny fingers. I swung my head, hair flying, and sang with Melba Moore from *Purlie*, my father's favorite, about the black preacher in the racist South who wants a new kind of life for his family: *I got love, I got love, I got love, love, love, love, love, love, love, love, love!* Or I'd sit in the kitchen, eating sliced apples and cheddar cheese while my mother deboned a chicken, or on my parents' bed with her, watching Mike Douglas and eating a salad of chopped iceberg lettuce, deep red tomato wedges, canned albacore tuna, thin rectangles of Jack cheese, and Catalina dressing. But when my parents were together in the same room, it was hard to maintain the fantasy of being part of the perfect family unit we desperately wanted.

When my mother became pregnant with their fourth child, if you counted Jeffrey, my father was distraught and advocated for an abortion. The two girls were enough, especially with me, a seven-year-old who shook her parents awake to make sure they weren't dead. Who called her father at work collect—since it was in another town—from the principal's office to see if there had been any deaths in the family.

Nevertheless, Sarah Kate Silverman emerged on December 1, 1970, a tiny white thing with a shock of black hair. It was to be the first shock of many, and the mildest. I dove for the phone when my father called from the hospital with the news. I fiddled with the coiled phone cord, praying it was a boy. "It's a bo . . . *girl!*" he teased.

My parents had been savvy enough at the start of this new decade to seek out a hospital where my mother could be awake for the birth and my father could be present. Also, where my mother would not be given an injection that would dry up her breast milk. To the dismay of all four grandparents—who thought of it as low-class, "like a Russian peasant"—my mother would actually breast-feed her new baby.

Watching the birth was apparently so moving that Donald tossed his pack of cigarettes on the desk of the nurses' station on his way out. "I won't be needing these anymore," he said, and he never smoked again. Although he still enjoyed the smell of ciga-rette smoke, he became indignant when people smoked in closed, populated places. In one memorable incident at an upscale restau-rant, he asked some diners at the next table to stop smoking. They stared at him blankly before resuming their conversation and ciga-rettes, blowing plumes of smoke in his direction. On the way out, he stopped at their table. "Suck on this for a while," he said, turned his backside to them, and farted loudly.

Sarah Kate came home, black and white and pooping. We called her Skunky until she was four. Sarah was our plaything. By the age of two, she regularly recited a list of swear words our father taught her: *bitch-bastard-damn-shit!* Her red lips formed a wide smile around perfect rows of tiny white teeth, her eyes like stage lights, her black bangs and ear-length bob framing her pale face like velvet stage curtains. We were captivated, in love, in awe. She was the world's cutest ventriloquist's dummy, sitting on Daddy's lap as she swore for appalled and delighted guests.

As Sarah approached nursery school age, her arm and leg hair began to look like our great-grandma's eyebrows—black and sprawling against pale white skin. Laura feared that the kids would make fun of her, so we took to petting Sarah's legs, repeating, af-firming, "Your fur is so *beautiful.*"

Sarah looked down at her limbs and grinned. "*Boo-di-ful!*"

Maybe the fur prompted the game Laura and I made for her. We'd throw one of Laura's drumsticks down the bedroom hallway and yell, "Fetch, Pizza! Fetch!" Sarah, a.k.a Pizza-the-Dog, would scurry down the hall on all fours in her stretchy little flowered Danskin pants, puffed by the diaper she wore even at four years old, and come back with the stick in her mouth.

Sarah continued to wet her bed for a famously long time, but Laura also found peeing significant, just in a different way. She stopped wetting the bed very young. But by the first grade she held empty toilet paper rolls like a penis to direct her pee into the bowl (or into the bushes if we were outdoors for a neighborhood kickball game). She wore boys' pants and shirts, even a suit and tie at formal gatherings. I admired Laura's boyishness and was tickled pink, so to speak, when people believed she was "Ryan" or "Kyle" or "Chris," the latter in honor of Chris Partridge of the singing sitcom family—a drummer like her. Friends and family criticized my mother for allowing Laura's behavior. They whispered *lesbian*, but my mother was unwavering in her support. She sensed that Laura's desire was better expressed than repressed. My father had no problem with Laura's behavior. *Fuck 'em* he said about anyone who tsk'ed at Laura's hair and clothes and rotating names. She was an excellent student, a nice kid, no hassle. She could wear what she wanted.

It didn't take a séance with Freud to guess that Laura was allowing the child she had replaced to become the boy he might have been. A boy I continued to wonder about. I often calculated the age Jeffrey would have been, and asked him in my head to give me a sign, maybe in a dream, that he was somehow still there.

Chapter 4

Who's Richer Than Us?

*M*y parents bought five acres of land on a narrow country road in nearby, rural Bedford, New Hampshire, and built their dream house. Night after night in the ranch house in which they had lived for most of their marriage, they sat with their architect, Donald LaValee—*Donald La-Valee, La-Valee so loooowwww* my mother liked to croon—and charted out a better life, one room at a time.

There was lots of light, with an art studio loft for my mother that looked out upon the high-ceiling living room as if from a balcony. *Wherefore art thou, Romeo?*

Wildflowers grew across the land. There was an, admittedly very shallow, narrow creek across the length of the land, and my mother bought a willow sapling for the top of the driveway to justify her romantic name for our new fantasy home: Willow Creek Farm. "Beth Ann's so-called creek looks more like someone took a piss," my father loudly announced as he and his best friend,

Arnold, surveyed the grounds through the glass door of the family room.

We girls got to choose motifs for our rooms: Mine was strawberry fields. I was orthodox in my décor—only strawberry anything was allowed. White walls with strawberry art. My mother painted red berries and green vines on my white dresser and bought strawberry throw pillows for the two twin beds. Laura's theme was Little House on the Prairie, with rough wood walls and calico bedding. Sarah's was colorful circles and balloons, popping primary colors.

My mother insisted on putting in a dumbwaiter that was like a tiny elevator going from the garage up to the kitchen. We used it with glee for the bags of groceries we unloaded from mom's station wagon. I'd summon it with a button and hold my breath. It arrived with a light thud. Was that a heavier thump than usual? With a tad of trepidation I opened the door and peered in to confirm that no crumpled dead body had been stashed there.

Other than the dumbwaiter, there was little opportunity for me to imagine dead bodies (sure, closed shower curtains, a walk-in pantry) in our large contemporary home on a hill at the back of the land. Giant windows faced a grassy expanse, featuring a tiny stream that trickled across it to a trout-stocked pond we could skate on in winter. We bought two horses and a pony—all older animals—to take us kids for galloping adventures along a quiet dirt road. The barn by the road dwarfed my mother's baby willow tree. It was originally yellow, but my parents had it painted storybook-red. When we had first moved to the new house, one of the men painting the tall slanted barn roof slipped. My mother saw it from our living room's picture window as he slid the full length of the smooth silver roof, flailing for something to latch onto, finally plummeting thirty feet to the ground. He was, amazingly, unhurt.

If ever there was a place where miracles could happen, and our Happy Family would emerge, this was it.

We were a great show. I had horses and a red barn and the funniest father ever, who would say things my friends' parents would never utter! My friend Ellen spent much of a summer with us, entertained by my father's craziness. *Hey, did you ever hear the Norfolk University cheer?* he'd ask. *We don't drink, we don't smoke, Noooor fuk!* Ellen laughed so hard she fell off her chair.

Scenic white ducks, important props in our display, floated peacefully on our reflective pond while concealing a muddy, catfish-filled pit beneath. Our dog, PD (after our dad, Philip Donald), chased down the ducks and killed them one by one, proudly dumping each carcass on our front steps. My father in his T-shirt and denim overalls would tie the latest dead duck to PD's collar in hopes of breaking him of this habit, but it didn't take. When the final duck succumbed, we headed out to buy a new bunch.

My parents were so disdainful of religion that they once jokingly threatened to punish me when I confessed to believing in God, but our new house was so Americana perfect that one Christmas, we even had Christmas. We decorated the tall pine with lights, ripping apart boxes of ornaments like presents on Christmas morning. Mom made a Star of David out of aluminum foil and placed it at the top. "You're not going to eat Santa's cookies, are you?" I asked my father sarcastically before bed.

"What do I look like, a schmuck?" he said.

I breathed in the sight: blazing fire, blinking lights, big Star of David, Daddy in his favorite sponge chair with Laura on his lap. Outside, snowflakes glimmering in the night sky, a white flurry of hope.

But there was no Christmas miracle for this bunch of Jews. On a Sunday morning after New Year's Day 1977, my parents sat the three of us girls on the couch after breakfast and shut off the television. "Mommy and I are getting a divorce," said my father before breaking into sobs.

Laura joined his crying. "Why?" she wailed.

"Because Mommy doesn't want me anymore," he said through his tears. My mother remained dry-eyed.

Sarah, who had been jumping along to the music on a television show, stood motionless and started to cry. *Oh baby!* we all called to her. *Come here! We love you! Everything will be okay!*

"I'm not crying because of *that*," Sarah said. "I'm crying because I was dancing and no one was watching me!"

I sat with my crying father, feeling strangely content. Finally, at age fourteen, I wasn't just needy—but needed. That same day, he moved into the house he had quietly bought the previous week, a place as dark and dank as my mother's was bright and uplifting. One of my horses, Dakota, died soon thereafter. My father, not one to let go of anything, mocked my mother's dreamy "Willow Creek Farm" by naming his cramped, smelly split-level "Dakota's Dead House."

Thinking back to the falling painter as I moved out of that house on a hill, I wondered—which part of this story was the omen? That the painter fell? Or that, miraculously, he was left unharmed? Perhaps it was both: He fell a long way but lived to tell the tale.

As my parents worked toward a custody agreement, my father kept a desperate chart of how many nights Laura, Sarah, and I stayed at his house. "Look at this, last week you were here four days and the other two were here three days," he'd say, showing me the check marks he'd made in his telltale green roll-tip pen. His theory was that he could get custody based on a mathematical formula involving the average number of sleepovers. "The Oedipus Complex works in my favor," he said. "As Laura and Sarah become teenagers they'll reject your mother and come to me."

My job as the oldest was to persuade my sisters to come to Daddy's house so that he could literally chalk it up. With my father depending on me, I was ruthless in my efforts. Guilt: "Daddy needs you!" Logic (which was illogical, because it wasn't true): "Mom's crazy and it's not healthy for you to stay there!" Hostility: "You're selfish. You only care about being in a nicer house."

Laura refused to succumb to the emotional blackmail. "Jesus," my dad would say to me in a big exhale. "Your mother could take a shit in the middle of the road, and Laura would defend her."

I brought this directly back to my sibling. "Laura, Mom could take a shit in the middle of the road, and you'd still defend her," I said.

Laura shrugged.

My sisters were more comfortable in their own rooms at Mom's, where life wasn't a contest scored in green ink on a yellow legal pad. I always made sure to give my dad at least one more day per week than my mom, which meant a night a week away from my sisters, but that was okay. I loved my alone time with my dad.

"You know, honey," my father said during one of our frequent evening walks around the neighborhood. "Papa is a wonderful grandfather to you, but he was so mean to me growing up. He hit me and called me stupid practically every day. He never once said he was proud of me. I'm better than Papa was and someday, when you're a mother, you'll be better than I am."

I squeezed his hand as we walked on, our boots scraping the icy road, our faces stinging in the cold.

"Listen, dahlin'," he continued, "it's really okay if you don't want to, but would you consider moving in with me? You know, where you'd keep your stuff here, and I would be your official home, and you'd pack to go visit your mom."

Simply by moving a few things, by making this little change, I could rescue my father from his untethered life. Amid all the bad things that could happen in the world, I could do something to fix this one. In that moment, a thin veil of the multi-layered cloak of anxiety that always hung around me, a sense of complete helplessness, lifted.

I carried my little black-and-white TV down the stairs of my mother's house, the antennae poking my face. *She's taking all her stuff*, I heard my mom say quietly to her friend Pat, who held my mom's hand as they stood together at the bottom of the stairs. Then she crumpled into Pat's arms. "It's just like when Jeffrey died."

It took a few years for my parents to get themselves together and create themselves anew. We became a sprawling, unconventional, and finally happy family. My parents built lives for themselves that worked. My mother went to a local college and got her degree in art education and married her philosophy professor, John O'Hara, a tall, straight-backed, bearded ex-Marine philosopher, the chair of the Humanities Department. Mom had easily earned all As, except for the B+ in John's class.

"Hey, what was that about?" we later teased him.

"That's what she deserved," he said in his deep, resonant voice, his diction as precise as our mother's.

John, quiet and self-contained, let us take the lead, and for a few years he was a fixture, a neutral presence in his easy chair, doing the *New York Times* crossword puzzle or reading a mystery novel. It took us by surprise when Laura, fifteen years old and furious at Mom, started to punch her, and John stood up, grabbed Laura's wrists in one large hand, and pushed her down to a sitting position on the stairs. When Laura told me about the incident, I was indignant, which was so much more satisfying than reflection.

"No, Susie," she corrected me. "He was right. I was hurting Mom, and he protected her. He put me in my place, and I belonged there."

After that, I began to take more notice of John. He was gentle and strong, knew everything, and was funny in an understated way.

Mom's love was theater. She got a small grant from the college to produce a play, which in turn led to the creation of a company, the New Thalian Players, which grew and thrived over thirty years into an award-winning regional theater. She begged John to take many of the singing parts—he had a beautiful, heartrending tenor—which he did out of his bottomless love for her, since he did not normally enjoy performing outside the occasional Christmas choir.

With John, Mom was not the wife who succeeded or failed in her duties. She was a person, his partner in life. Mom directed her plays; John taught his classes. She cooked dinner; he cooked dinner. He did the dishes; she did the dishes. There was no keeping score. No resentment, blame, or complaint. Marriage was not a zero-sum game. Each of them was good at some things and less so at others, and that was okay.

My father, meanwhile, became less judgmental and met the love of his life. Technically, he had met Janice twenty-odd years earlier when they shared a dance at her cousin's bar mitzvah, but when she was visiting her parents in Massachusetts for a summer, a childhood friend called my father and said, "My cousin Janice is here and you're going to take her out."

"That's nuts," my father told him. "She lives in California."

"Donald," said Milton, who was over seven feet tall and beefy. "I'm not asking."

My father and Janice fell in love. She extended her stay a week before flying back to her job selling magazine advertising in Marin County, and throughout the early fall I could hear my dad talking and laughing on the phone from behind the closed door of his room.

In October, Janice visited, and my sisters and I met her over Middle Eastern food at The Cedars of Lebanon in Manchester. She was definitely a new specimen of woman, different not only from our mom but from every mom we had ever met. She had long, silky blonde hair. Sarah, who was six, grabbed it, unable to resist the shiny smoothness, and it came off in her hand. We stared, dumbstruck, waiting for the apocalypse, but Janice merely pinned the fall back onto her real hair. She sported long, manicured fingernails painted "fuchsia," which sounded to me like a combination of "fuck" and "puke." When the thick yogurt in which we were dipping our pita bread got caught under her nails, she delicately licked them clean. I wondered if they, too, might come off.

We fell in love with her.

My father took me to San Francisco in November to meet Janice's seven-year-old daughter, Jodyne. She was adorable, with a face like a chipmunk: buck teeth, dimples, sad brown eyes. We claimed each other immediately as sisters, and I was desperate to prove it. Jody came home from school angry about a neighbor girl who had teased her.

We went outside and found the girl straddled over her bike. "Leave my little sister alone," I said, the epitome of a teenage sister. "Or you'll deal with me."

While Jody went to her father for Thanksgiving, Janice, Dad and I had dinner with old friends from New Hampshire who had moved to the Bay Area. My father tried to talk sense into their thirteen-year-old son, a heavy pot smoker, arguing the legal and health risks and about not compromising his mind and faculties. "What's so great about it, anyway?" my dad said.

"Why don't you try it and see?"

That Thanksgiving, we all sat around smoking pot. We laughed nonstop. My father ate an entire pecan pie. My eyes widened at the sight of Janice using her manicured fingernails as a roach clip.

They day before we flew home, my father took Jody for a walk, and Janice and I had alone time. "I never met a guy who loves his kids like your dad," she told me. "He's something special. But, between you and me, he has to get rid of those overalls." Funny, wearing overalls was the one thing my parents had in common.

The family that emerged was not made in our blood, but felt in our bones. Not a whole cloth, but patches and seams. Only after we stopped holding our nuclear family together, desperately smearing ourselves in some sort of emotional superglue, only when we let the pieces fall apart, were we able to build something real. We were a mosaic—or, perhaps, Mosaic.

The story of Moses descending Mount Sinai, catching the Israelites in the act of idolatry, and smashing the tablets, is well known. Less well known is after Moses later brought the new, whole tablets to the people, and they carried on with their journey, they took the whole tablets—and the smashed ones—with them. Like for the Israelites, carrying our brokenness gave us truth, dynamism, and purpose.

My family also carried our broken pieces with us. They lend us gratitude and pride. My father, wrapping his arm around John's shoulder, looks around the Thanksgiving table at our big unwieldy family. "Who's richer than us?" he asks. "No one, I'll tell you. This is as good as it gets."

"I do believe you are right this time, Donald," John replies.

Chapter 5

Mount Sinai, Addis Ababa, and Johnny Cash

*I*n October 1999, I sent out an email to my three sisters: "Who wants to pay for her own ticket and come be my servant and helper for a week in Ethiopia? Reward: Meet your new nephew and help bring him home!" Jody responded within the hour. She would fly with me to meet my son, just as I had flown to meet her when she was about to become my sister, when she was seven and still living in San Francisco with Janice.

During the twelve-hour flight to Addis Ababa, Jody, a documentary film editor for *National Geographic*, had her first sip of the strongest, muddiest coffee she had ever tasted. "God, no wonder Ethiopians win marathons," she exclaimed, and launched into a furious pantomime, using only her hands, of biking, swimming, running, jumping jacks, and, well, high-speed nose picking. She is rightly famous in our family for these frenetic gestures, ever since the age of ten when, using only her upper body, she dramatized how I had cleaned up the house after a big party I'd thrown while our parents were away for the weekend: picking marijuana roaches out of the electric burners of the stove, sniffing the rugs for beer, and looking under the beds for unseemly remnants of drunken teenagers. A gentleman we had met on the plane looked at us with an eyebrow-scrunching frown that indicated he was withdrawing the invitation to dinner at his home he had so recently extended.

The wheels hit the tarmac. The plane slowed and stopped. The redemptive ding sounded that meant we could remove our seat belts. The sound of Johnny Cash wafted over the speakers.

I'm stuck in Folsom Prison

And time keeps dragging on

"Country music?" Jody said, as if detecting a gas leak. "On Ethiopian Airlines?"

In fact, the smell of diesel followed us into the terminal and throughout the drive to the hotel. It was the smell of the city—which, at five in the morning, was quiet and gray. There were rows of shacks made of what looked like mud, straw and corrugated metal. Some were shops; others were homes. Cars with missing headlights wove among the few people out at dawn. Most of them were carrying bunches of kindling wrapped to their backs with swaths of cloth.

Our driver, Samuel, expertly maneuvered the streets in his battered, gray two-door Ford. He was handsome and young—maybe twenty-three—with dreadlocks. He was a cousin of Yosef's friend Ashegre, an Ethiopian Coptic Christian who managed the compound in Addis Ababa that housed a Jewish community waiting to move to Israel. He helped maintain the school, organize food distribution, arrange medical care, and manage the on-site industry of embroidering challah covers and prayer shawls.

The rising sun was a red glow when the manicured lawns and marble statues of the Addis Ababa Sheraton appeared like Oz before us. A Saudi royal had built the hotel to give Addis Ababa a symbol of wealth and glory, and it was palatial—dark marble, with gold-rimmed glass doors and windows. There were flower gardens and a pool. A roof soared over the circular driveway, and doormen in red, broad-shouldered jackets with gold tassels opened the doors for us with a smile. I thought of my friend Paul, a poet and novelist, who worked as a doorman during summer breaks from college. People are not necessarily who they seem. Wide stretches of marble flooring glimmered and carpeted staircases with gold handrails swung upward around the foyer like grand shawls on a queen.

"I can't believe this place," I said, embarrassed in front of Samuel by the display of affluence. "This is the fanciest hotel I've ever seen."

I must have rambled, because Jody stopped me. "Susie, enough," she whispered.

We got to our room a little after five in the morning, and fell into deep sleep, facing each other across the lush king-sized bed. The rabbis teach that throughout the encampments around Mount Sinai, the night before making their covenant with God, the Israelites slept a deep, unconscious sleep. God wanted them to go straight from bed to receive the Torah—the original come-as-you-are party—with their analytical skills still dozing, so that the experience was unmediated by what another Jewish guy, centuries later, would call superego. I hoped I could release my own self-consciousness when I approached the orphanage and met my son for the first time.

Even before the wake-up call from the front desk, Jody and I simultaneously opened our eyes with a start. "*I hear the train a-comin'* . . . " Jody started to sing. Johnny Cash was our theme music.

"Everything will be alright, right?" I asked my sister, suddenly serious.

"Oh, Sooz," Jodyne said with a squeeze on my arm. "We'll love him immediately."

"What about Yosef and the girls. They're okay, right?" I had a scene in my head. Two shoppers at Whole Foods, both acquaintances of ours, talking in the aisle. Piles of organic produce in their carts. Starbucks mugs in the cup-holders. *Can you imagine? Her whole family killed here in Newton at the same moment she's meeting their new son in Ethiopia . . . Just terrible.*

On our way to the parking lot to meet Samuel, Jody gasped and pointed up to our left. What we thought in the early dawn light to be lush, green rolling hills spattered with lovely white villas was really a painted mural—a three-story billboard blocking the mass of gray, dilapidated shanties spread far and wide behind it. As we drove through the gate, I saw a man with only one leg sitting in the dirt. Rain began to fall, as if the sky could not be such a bright blue over this misery. I reached to the back seat for Jody's hand.

There were no stoplights or crosswalks. Pedestrians, drivers, cows, donkeys, and goats all aggressively negotiated their way through streets and intersections. I closed my eyes as we sped toward whatever happened to be crossing the road in front of us, wanting also to shut out the terrifying randomness of it all.

"The streets no have names," Samuel explained as he pulled to the side of the road. "This is the right neighborhood, but now we must find the street." He called out to two adolescent boys for directions. They smiled broadly and tried out their English: "Hello, Hello!" One climbed into the front seat with me, the other in the back with Jody, who laughed at their unfiltered exuberance. They directed Samuel with words and gestures, occasionally turning to me and Jody to say, "America, America," or, "America good." They laughed and elbowed each other, and got out of the car on a quiet street in front of a high, rusty fence. Samuel beeped the horn, puncturing the quiet, and a man with white hair, who looked to be in his sixties, in gray trousers and a blue and gray sweater, slid open the wide, heavy gate. There before us was the African Cradle Children's Center.

My whole life had led to this place. Yet, I didn't even know how to open the car door, or how to greet the exuberant children who ran to our car in joyful greeting. I was awed by their smiles and voices, their beckoning. I was afraid Samuel wouldn't come back to get us, and I'd be stuck at the orphanage forever. I was terrified that I wouldn't love my son. Or even recognize him. I imagined myself standing there, dressed like Mrs. Banks, the mother in *Mary Poppins*: a nineteenth-century lady with a large white hat, ruffled blouse, and billowing skirt. "Such dear orphans, poor things. I shall pat them each on the head." I would look around frantically, unable to discern one brown child from another, my claim as a mother exposed: white American economic privilege.

Hiking up my loose, light-blue cotton dress, I mounted the two-foot stone platform that ran the length of the front wall. How obvious is it that I'm accustomed to proper stairs and doors and countless other comforts? How vain was I to imagine everyone in that compound analyzing my every move? I was the epitome of writer Anne Lamott's twin phrases: "a narcissist with an inferiority complex" and "the piece of shit around which the world revolves."

Okay, Susan. Stop. Breathe. Get out of your own head. I was about to live the story I would tell and re-tell my growing son. *When I first laid eyes on you I knew . . .* God brought us together? You were mine? I was a fraud?

A smiling woman opened the door before I could knock. She was holding a baby girl swaddled in a ruffled pink fleece onesie. "Hallo," she said. "I am Fitsum. I take care of the children here."

I smiled back. "I'm Susan," I said, trying to convey perfect-mother-ness. Joyful yet calm. Enthusiastic yet composed.

Narcissistic yet insecure.

I peered beyond her into the orphanage. The room was spotless, lined with white cribs. A toddler played on a woven rug in the center of the room with a woman who handed her plastic shapes. As we smiled awkwardly at each other Fitsum made no move to allow me through the rusted doorway. Why wasn't she showing me in, leading me to Adar? Was I supposed to greet her in a specific way? Was I missing a customary saying or gesture that would let me into the inner sanctum, past these final, aching moments, to be with the son I had kept in my heart and would now finally hold in my arms? His soft cheeks, the feel of his breath, the weight of his body in my arms were so close that the magnetic force—the invisible tug that reached across an ocean and drew me to this one doorway, the way God brought the Israelites from slavery to Sinai—cast an irresistible pull. Why wasn't she letting me get by?

Finally Fitsum raised the child in her arms toward me. "This is your baby," she said, just this side of bemused.

"But . . . " I looked in confusion at the baby, all in pink.

Then I took in his face, the slight uplift of his eyebrows forming a peak above his nose, the "o" of his lips as he solemnly studied my face.

Adar.

I could feel Jody stifling a smirk behind me as I took my baby into my arms. Adar or, perhaps, still Daniel, twisted his body away from me and reached for Fitsum. Her eyes, like his, were shiny black and watery. Then Adar turned to me, and I kissed his forehead. He smelled like sour milk. His skin was covered in red bumps. He looked at me weirdly.

Who was I? A person alienated by my own child's smell! Xenophobes—*racists*—talk about "others" in olfactory terms, and here I was already looking forward to transforming my own son with a warm, sudsy bath in the refuge of the hotel, in the opulence of the Addis Ababa Sheraton, where orphans and poverty would be relegated to the more comfortable realm of theory. Where I could call Yosef and hear him say that everything was okay. I wondered if the hotel room had cable; I could use an American sitcom before bed. Fran Drescher's nanny assuring the three motherless children that, yes, their father pays her to take care of them, but she loves them from her heart.

Fitsum led us into the large, open room. Jody and I glanced around. A baby around Adar's age stood at the end of a crib and reached out to us. A toddler on the floor banged a plastic ball in my direction. At the back wall, beside the last crib, three women sat at a low children's table on small plastic chairs like the ones at Hallel's preschool. They wore clean, light-blue housecoats over dresses, their black hair pulled back into buns. With a spoon or bottle in one hand and a child in the other arm, they fed their charges with expert efficiency and soothing words. Seeing that they were not covered in baby food or struggling to keep the children still made me feel even more inadequate. The Israelites may have received the Torah in a guileless, rubbing-the-sleep-from-their-eyes state, but I received my son with self-consciousness—more guarded and awkward in my actions before these caregivers than the Israelites were before God. Pointing at me while looking into Adar's face, Fitsum said, "Mama, Mama," and slowly backed away. Adar whimpered and scrunched his brows in deep concern. My heart was breaking along with his. And with hers. "I

had a baby boy at the same time Daniel was brought in," Fitsum
would later tell me. "My son was my baby at night, but Daniel
was my baby in the day."

Fitsum would be the closest person to a birth mother for Adar
we would ever know—the woman who held, cared for, and loved
him for his first nine months, starting just days after the police had
found him, a newborn alone on an Addis Ababa street. No other
information about him had been known or recorded. Had he been
wrapped in a blanket? Placed in a basket?

Jody patted Adar's back. I steadied myself with a hand on hers.
Thank God she had come to Ethiopia with me.

"What if this *isn't* Adar?" I whispered, even though I knew it
was. I had carried his photos for eight months, since the day the
agency sent them to us when he was a couple of months old. I
could have described each picture from memory: the angle of his
lips (a range from knowingly crooked smile to pursed to casually
parted), the intensity of his eyes, the arch of his eyebrows ("It's
cute that you're jingling those bells, but I'll smile for you in any
case").

"This baby is pretty like a girl," I said, turning him to face Jody.

"It's him, Sooz. Don't worry."

I looked at him face-to-face and said, baby-voiced, "We're
gonna make sure YOU have a penis."

"Your first words to your son," Jody said dreamily. "Should I
write them in his baby book?"

Adar raised his eyebrows curiously at me in the Photo No. 4,
"Oh, please" expression as we laid him on the large braided rug in
the center of the room. I tried to look nonchalant, and non-
pedophile, as I pulled open the waistband of his fleecy pink pants
and peeked under the frayed cloth diaper with the bent safety pins.
I wanted to be overjoyed, full of love, completely surrendered to

the covenantal moment, but instead I was nervously checking for a penis.

"This is the first uncircumcised penis I've ever seen," I whispered to my sister. "Well, sober."

I picked up my baby and kissed him. Amid all the suffering I had seen—just in our drive from the hotel to the orphanage—how could I be silly and joking? I should be railing at God, reaching a new low of shaken faith, embracing my father's lifelong theology: *If there's a God, He's an asshole.* I had lived my life in terror of the kind of loss that surrounded me now like the sea: dead parents, dead children. But for the first time in my whole life no voice in my head negotiated with God. No begging voices clamored to bargain or fight for anything, or demand that a capricious Ruler pay attention. I simply engaged in my end of the deal with the Creator-of-the-World in this one country, this one neighborhood, this one building, and with this one boy, to make a little order. Throughout my life and then eventually through my Jewish education that, frankly, only started in rabbinical school, I had alternately rebuked and implored God, despaired of and celebrated tradition, lorded my own righteousness over some teachings and stood in humility and even shame before the vastness and depth of the tradition. But now, my sister, my new son, the caregivers, and the children in this orphanage with me comprised a microcosm of love, tragedy, hope, apathy, brokenness, and healing—the shattered and the whole—the promise of Sinai.

And in it I wasn't God's judge or God's bitch. I was God's partner.

Jody crinkled her nose. I took Adar over to the changing table and pulled his soft little legs out of his pants. I worried that I was overstepping by helping myself to the facilities without asking permission but, with the language barrier, neither did I want to seem like I was telling a caregiver to change him for me. I unfastened the safety pins and removed the rag that served as a diaper. There was a basket on my left that had a few other soiled items in it, and I threw this one in too. Fitsum came over, took a fresh rag, dipped it in the bucket of water to my right, and handed it to me. For a moment, we both held the same threadbare cloth, and exchanged a smile.

As I cleaned the extreme mess, which seemed to indicate some sort of parasite in Adar's body, I saw how red, rashed and raw he was. Despite the sores, he didn't cry at my touch. I cleaned him slowly and gently, looking into his eyes and repeating his old and new names, *Dani, Adar, Dani, Adar,* using just a corner of the rag before rinsing it in the increasingly dirty bucket of water. I kissed his forehead, cheeks, and tummy. Freshly diapered, I picked him up just as a woman came over with a baby about Adar's age. I handed Adar to Jody and took the baby from the woman, who seemed a little surprised, but I was on a roll—I'd help out. This baby, too, was covered in sores. I dipped a fresh rag into the same water bucket and, stifling gags from the mess in her diaper, cleaned her up. Adari's dirty diaper hadn't bothered me at all, I realized with satisfaction. My covenant was with him. He was my son.

Finished, I turned to Adar and we took each other in. He arched his eyebrows and granted me a half smile as I spoke my first baby book–worthy words to him, a phrase oft repeated in my family.

"You are mine forever."

Chapter 6

Rose

I have always wanted to adopt, even when I was a child with a penchant for writing poetry instead of going out for recess.

She looked to the stars / And wondered / Someday / Will I find my mother?

"Who is the little girl in your poem?" asked Miss Loros as I hovered beside her desk, where she was focused on correcting a pile of math quizzes.

"She's an orphan," I said. "Someday I want to be the mother of orphans."

"Then you'd be dead," she pointed out, not taking her eyes off her flow of check and *X* marks.

At the end of fourth grade, while my mother was drying a wooden salad bowl with a dishtowel, I made an announcement. "Mommy, when I grow up I'm going to adopt a hundred children, one from every country." Two long, straight braids framed my face, and my orange gauze shirt was embroidered with flowers dotted with tiny silver mirrors.

"That's a wonderful idea," my mom said. She turned and placed her cool, still damp fingers under my chin. "Even adopting one child would be a beautiful thing."

That was two years after I had said good-bye to Rose.

Rose was my sister. Or, she felt like one. She was a child from the foster care system who lived with us for a year, and who left us as suddenly as she had arrived.

When I was six, Laura was three, and Sarah was not yet even a glimmer, my parents announced that we were to have a new sister: Rose Rollins, aged nine. This was right, because she was three years older than I, just the way I was three years older than Laura, and someone coming into our family was the opposite of my fears.

"Where are her mommy and daddy?" I asked.

"She doesn't live with them anymore," said my mother. "They have very sad problems, so they can't take care of Rose or her brothers and sisters."

In my heart I had made her my sister so quickly I was even a little jealous that I might have to share her with those other siblings—"six of them, I think," said my mother—each of whom had been parceled out among different families. I pictured a husband and wife standing on a farmhouse porch, sadly waving good-bye as their seven hungry children were driven off in a dog-catcher's van.

Laura had a different reaction. "I don't want her."

Instinctively, my parents wanted all the children of the world to have a warm family and the companionship of siblings. "Our friend Selma works for Children's Services and she told them we would be a good family for a child who needs one," my mother explained. "Rose needs love and we have plenty of it." My father had been berated by his father and never protected by his mother. His brother sailed under the radar by obeying and succeeding at home and in school, but Donald smoked cigarettes, failed his classes, and broke his leg trying to ride the garage door. Meanwhile, my mother and her sister, Martha, fell asleep each night holding hands between their two single beds, a force united against their mother's constant criticism and their father's helplessness in the face of it.

Rose arrived within the week. She was pretty and a bit plump, with black hair and blue eyes. We took her to see where she would sleep, a former guest room whose twin beds were covered in white lacy bedspreads.

"Ooh, this is so pretty," she cooed. She placed her clothes neatly in the dresser. Then she turned and considered me. "You know, if you tucked your shirt in, you'd look like a teenager." She repositioned my IZOD shirt, and I could already imagine her sticking up for me in the playground (not that this had been a problem) and helping me with homework (not that I did any).

At the dinner table that first night, Rose sat between Laura in her booster seat and my father in his jacket and loosened tie. "Mom, would you please pass the pork chops?" she said. "Dad, would you like some broccoli?" My parents froze mid-bite, but Rose continued to eat—fast and a lot.

After dinner, Laura and I huddled in the tub at bath time as our mother shampooed our heads. Rose was big enough to shower by herself.

"She eats a lot," Laura said.

My mother made sure the hallway was clear before explaining to us that Rose had spent years competing with six brothers and sisters for not enough food.

I looked for proof that Rose was mine, and found it where I could. In Miss Abbott's first-grade class, on the white lined paper reserved for our best penmanship, I carefully wrote the names of the people in my family, oldest to youngest—Daddy, Mom, Rose,

Susie, Laura. To fight the nagging sense that this new sister wasn't real, I took pleasure in nestling "Rose" safely in the middle.

She and I both loved horses, and when my father included her in the family pass he bought to the annual Deerfield Fair, that seemed to clinch it. My father was a stickler for fairness and wouldn't have included Rose if she weren't part of the family! Rose and I rode over and over, getting off at the end of three trots around the ring and running straight back to stand in line again. Laura threw baseballs into holes like a pro. I got off the Tilt-A-Whirl dizzy and pretended to be drunk: "Hey lady, how d'ya get your eyes to spin in your head like that!" We all shot at rubber ducks in booths, hesitantly fed the goats, and doggedly ate fried dough. After our baths that night, Rose and I sat on the end of her bed with the door closed. She pulled a hard, sticky candied apple from her purse and carefully peeled off the clear plastic wrap. I liked the candy coating, and Rose liked the apple, so she suggested I nibble off the outside and she'd eat the rest.

If she ate an apple that I had bitten all over, that was proof that we were a family.

Mom brought us to Concord to have lunch with Nana who worked part-time in the store, as she had for twenty-five years. After lunch, Nana took us to the toy store next door and had us each choose what we wanted. I helped Laura find a coloring book before hitting the games section: Candy Land, check. Monopoly, check. Chutes and Ladders, check. Operation, check. What didn't I already have? Rose followed sheepishly, and Nana had to insist that she get something for herself.

"Maybe she doesn't want anything," I whispered to my Nana.

"You know, Susie," Nana said in a quiet voice, "when I was a girl my uncle was left with two little boys when his wife died. He married a woman with two children of her own. That woman was the only mother those little boys had, but she never loved them. She gave her own children money on Hanukkah, but not those poor boys, and I remember telling myself that I would never be like her."

One Saturday morning, nearly a year after Rose came to us, I was sitting on the den floor surrounded by colorful construction paper where I had been attempting to draw a frog on a lily pad. Rose was on the couch eating a bowl of cereal and watching cartoons. She was wearing new pajamas from Daddy's store—yellow babydolls with a white fringe. The bottoms were long and stretched tightly around one knee where it was folded beneath her. Her other leg dangled off the edge of the couch, her pink polish from Kmart peeling on her toenails.

Mom came and sat beside her, putting her hand on Rose's knee and nodding at me to leave the room.

My mother had told me what would happen, but I didn't really believe it. It didn't seem possible. "It's better for her to be near her brothers and sisters," she had said early that morning as we sat on her bed, her hand on my knee the way it rested on Rose's now. But what was I? Was I not her sister too? I lurked outside the door, catching glimpse of Rose's face falling as the news registered. She didn't look at the woman she had called Mom for almost a year, and neither of us could have known at the time that my mother was pregnant again. Choices had to be made. As I walked away, toward my bedroom, I heard the cartoon on the TV beep and trill in the background. *That's all, folks!*

My family was strangely quiet for the next few days, speechless. A godlike voice of rebuke silently filled the house. I didn't know where Rose was going the morning that my father loaded three huge, brand new suitcases into my mother's car. A luggage set seemed like such an odd gift for a nine-year-old. I was afraid to ask if she was going to live with one of her sisters at Webster House, a foster residence on a busy Manchester street across from a gas station, next to a superette that sold cigarettes, magazines covered in darkened plastic, and single cans of beer. Webster House was for children with no one to take care of them. Every time we drove past, I stared out the rear window to catch a glimpse of any child who lived there. I wondered what bedtime was like. Did children cry out in the night for their mothers? Did the grown-ups who worked there yell at them to shut up and go to sleep?

I took in the smell of gasoline that dripped from beneath my mother's car. Usually that smell, coupled with suitcases, meant a trip, maybe even Disney World, but today it smelled like drifting and desolation.

My father arranged the luggage in the back seat so Rose would have enough room. As long as that ride lasted, she would have a secure place in the world. When she walked past me out of the house, her head down, I wanted to hug her, but she held her arms close to her sides and seemed embarrassed—as if the music had stopped in a game of musical chairs and someone had pulled the seat out from under her.

She sat in the back seat of the car with a big plastic bag in her lap—bright yellow with a big orange poppy, the insignia of Daddy's store. I waved until the car was out of sight, as if offering a blessing, but she didn't look back.

Part 2

Chapter 7

Not in Heaven

*F*or our first date, Yosef wore his obscene cutoffs. I was freshly showered and draped in sexy-casual "bag-o-rags"—brightly colored swatches of gauze that came packaged in a net sack. I had twisted one piece around my top like a bikini, and tied two at my hips to create a flowing skirt. I also wore the confidence of someone with a good story to tell, because I had just spent the night in jail.

I had been handcuffed, fingerprinted, and locked up for protesting the US embargo on Nicaragua. Me, and five hundred others, but that did not dilute the power of my story. I was *authentic.*

But not as authentic as Yosef. He spoke without notes at divestment rallies. He answered reporters' questions with the ease of a well-informed visionary. I was an avid reader of his column, "Not the Weather," in which he addressed world affairs and moral obligations every week as I sat in the Speak Easy office, the peer-counseling center where I volunteered, and where I was always thankful that the phone never rang while I was there, because despite the trainings I had no idea how to handle it if someone ever came to me for help. As I sat at the bare black desk equipped with nothing but a rotary phone, a legal pad, and a pen, I would stare at his byline and photo while an occasional thought popped into my mind: *Maybe one day I'll marry this guy.*

I hadn't met him in person until the previous week at a Boston University library sit-in, where I had wanted to save the world but didn't know what to say in the press release I was supposed to bang out. The other protesters sat on the floor and linked arms, chanting *BU Divest or Continued Unrest,* while I sat apart from them, trying to draft the release before the police shut us down. They were already calling loudly through the bullhorns: *Evacuate the premises*!

"BU divest," I began to write. No, wait. How about: "We the students of Boston University . . . " *think racism isn't nice? Don't like apartheid?* If only I could splatter myself across the page—my passion, the thrill of the mission, the hearkening of my heart to cries of distress from the other side of the world. How our souls were in sync with the human desire for morality and goodness. We had heard the cries from Soweto and demanded that our university divest from South Africa. Then, in my black T-shirt with a mushroom cloud over a cemetery of RIP crosses, I could meet up with everyone at the Underground for a self-righteous beer.

There was a hand on my shoulder. I swiveled to find myself staring at cutoff jeans so short I had to jerk my head away. My gaze traveled upward past a T-shirt that read "Freedom Charter of South Africa" and on to shoulder-length light-brown hair, a blue-and-white knit yarmulke fastened to it by a silver clip. Yosef's eyes were unnaturally huge behind thick glasses in a dull silver frame.

"Here, let me do it," he said. "I have experience with these things."

What a pompous ass, I thought. However, I relinquished the rumpled sheet of paper with secret relief, and watched as this nerdy Jewish boy scribbled a few paragraphs and got them to the copy machine in under a minute.

I quickly found a place on the floor with the others in our state-of-the-art university library. I recognized students there from Howard Zinn's class, where we read Emma Goldman's *My Life* and Zinn's own *A People's History of the United States*. We were reading firsthand accounts of the civil rights and anti-war movements in which my professor had been a stalwart force. Back when I was listening to my parents' lonely objections to war in Manchester, New Hampshire, he had had the Pentagon Papers hidden in a locked drawer of his office at BU.

That this was a protest of privilege was not lost on me, but not all privilege is equal. "I've got my financial aid to worry about," said a girl to no one in particular as she made her way to the exit, jumping from one clear spot of floor to another across a river of hands, feet, and backpacks. "My parents will kill me if I lose my scholarship," another one said sheepishly as he gathered his things. Yosef, despite the risks—he was there on full scholarship—not only stayed, he addressed the police and the press.

Yosef and I hugged awkwardly on the Boston Common lawn. He was as skinny as the pen sticking out of the frayed pockets of his threadbare shorts, yet he faced the world with a commanding sense of purpose, taking it all in at high speed through his smudged glasses.

He laid out a frayed batik tapestry, rows of black elephants on light-brown weave. I was bursting to boast of my night in jail, but I hoped he wouldn't ask for details. I had no idea what the Nicaraguan Embargo was about. To this day I don't really understand the issue, but one of my goals before graduation had been to be arrested along with Howard Zinn, my teacher and mentor, and Howard was the one who had invited me to join the demonstration.

In the sun-dappled shade, eating the grapes Yosef had brought, I asked him if he was afraid that his activism would get him kicked out of school. By way of explanation, he said he had wanted to call his column "Not in Heaven," but the paper had made him change it because it was biblical, a line from Deuteronomy. God says that the Torah, the Five Books of Moses, is "not in heaven"—not above or beyond the people. It is in our hands to interpret and bring to life.

The world is our responsibility.

I had dreamt of this kind of passion-meets-reality since 1972, when I was nine and our house was filled with McGovern campaign workers. I'd plop myself on the couch, my long brown braids still damp and smelling of baby shampoo and cream rinse. Pulling my lanky legs onto the couch, I arranged my babydoll nightgown in a fan around me. "Nixon is willing to kill our boys," I parroted authoritatively. It was an early version of Reagan in Nicaragua—trusting the people I was with in lieu of actually learning about the issue and forming authentic opinions (although I probably would have come to the same conclusions).

Laura, sitting on our dad's legs in her pajama shorts with the cowboy print, was quiet, even shy. Her piercing, almond-shaped green eyes seemed to record every interaction, but she didn't mimic their words like I did. She watched and listened. "Laura, how do you suggest we end the war?" our father asked. A roomful of smiling faces fell on her, and she thought for a moment. "Maybe instead of putting bombs on the planes, they can put cookies. When they drop the cookies, people will be so happy they'll throw away their guns and run to go eat them."

Sarah was now two, with bangs and jet-black hair to her chin, and giant black eyes staring out of a round, pale monkey-face. She regularly performed her routine, sitting on our father's lap and surrounded by our houseful of volunteers from Boston, New York, Philadelphia, and Chicago. "Bitch, bastard, damn, shit," she said, courtesy of our father's early tutelage. All the McGovern campaign workers who lived with us—Jewish, black, Irish, Italian—couldn't get enough of my baby sister's mix of adorable and vulgar.

And so many of the volunteers were Jewish! It was a novelty for this New Hampshire girl. They slept everywhere and anywhere—couches, floors, even chairs. At night after my bath, I'd help my mother put out plates of food, bottles of soda, and ashtrays.

My father both relished and resented these guests who spent their days doing what he would have liked to do. "Hey, go ahead, have another beer," he'd say sarcastically. "I'll just restock it for you." But he also loved the company and passionate discussions with people who shared his views and values—a rare opportunity in his small-minded New Hampshire world. As the campaigners straggled in, my father changed from a suit into jeans with a striped V-neck whose collar ends were as pointy as weapons. He had long, heavy black sideburns and looked as cool as anyone when he sat in one of our two striped orange and beige sponge chairs shaped like giant space entities.

Formerly a stay-at-home mom, my mother had meanwhile rebuilt herself into George McGovern's photographer, traveling with him and taking Polaroids to leave with voters as keepsakes. She thrived among that crowd: discussing polls, strategies, unsavory Republican tactics, and sharing stories of days on the road with the candidate.

My sisters and I wove in and out, as Laura and I poured beer, absorbed the vibe, and took in the conversation: criticism of

Republican opposition to the Equal Rights Amendment, the exploitation of the poor, failures of the Civil Rights Act—and, most of all, The War and The Draft. I might not have understood the issues themselves, but I saw beyond the broken parts of my family, beyond my own fears, to the shattered world. I sensed an amorphous power around me and in me to help fix it. The energy—an upward, expanding whirl—was so great that it seemed impossible for McGovern to lose.

I loved these campaigners with their long hair and Levi's. Oh, how I wanted worn, patched jeans like theirs—the garb of the righteous! I felt lifted by a sense of purpose, a feeling I never got from school, sports, or Girl Scouts. These students who were "taking a semester off" seemed to be tapped into something bigger than politics. There was a glow of goodness and truth flickering in their words and in their work. A handsome college student with a gold front tooth would pull out his guitar. *This land is your land . . .*

Yosef, in the cutoff version of those jeans-of-justice, embodied the same sense of power and possibility. I found him irresistible, even though he didn't meet my wish list for a mate: he was average height, his parents were divorced, he proudly played the kazoo when I wanted to be serenaded with a guitar, and he wore a yarmulke when I had been taught that religion was for idiots.

My lips were chapped from my night in a dry cell, but still I hoped he would kiss me.

He did.

"My lips aren't usually like this," I said, apologizing.

"It's okay," he said.

The next school year, Yosef was a senior at BU while I was at Harvard Graduate School of Education. I helped him make divestment placards and place them in his window. When university maintenance was dispatched to take them down, we made new ones and taped them back up. After a few rounds, Yosef stationed himself outside his door wearing his prayer shawl, holding a prayer book, and singing softly.

"Let them move me," he said.

They didn't.

I argued against racism, sexism, and homophobia, but Yosef actually fought those things with vision and strategy. He believed that every person is made *b'tzelem elohim*, in the image of God. Who had ever heard of the commission to make Martin Luther King Day a national holiday? He had. Yosef was a national student representative on the commission. Who had ever heard of Alexei Magarik. Yosef had. He organized an international campaign and hunger strike to release Magarik from Soviet detention.

Yosef showed me that my ideological passions were rooted in timeless Jewish ideas. I in turn taught him that ideology is not enough—we need love, too. After he ignored me for days at a time, immersed in his studies and activism and not returning my calls, I would become anxious and desperate. Together again at last, I'd sing him a song from my youth, from *Hair. How can people be so heartless, how can people be so cruel? . . . especially people who care about strangers, who care about evil and social injustice . . .*

Sometimes we had Friday night dinner at the house of Yosef's father, Martin. Those were oasis moments for me, where Yosef and I were a couple in the context of an extended family, as opposed to the otherwise chaotic nature of our relationship—he, involved in issues and school and I, trying to find him, to pin him down for a time. Yosef's three-year-old sister, Miriam, climbed onto his lap and he taught her to say "communism." She ran back and forth between the dining room and the kitchen saying, "coh-moo-nism, coh-moo-nism." I thought of Sarah as a toddler reciting "bitch-bastard-damn-shit"—it still brought a smile to my face—but I liked this twist. It was funny *and* connected to big ideas.

When Martin first invited me to light the candles, I tried to hold steady but my hand shook. Again, Yosef was the real thing—engaged so naturally in the ritual—and I was the fake, the one who was arrested on behalf of the Sandinistas. Or was it against them? I lit the match and froze. Did I have to light the right or the left first? Did it matter? When do I start the blessing? Wasn't there something about covering my eyes? Yosef intuitively, in a whisper, took the lead, getting me off the hook again. The candle-lighting magic didn't feel like it belonged to me, but like grace, a little gift of light I serendipitously encountered. Yosef's family belonged to the flames and incantations, and the candles to them. The rituals were not sanctimonious or lofty, but part of dinner, just like laughter, conversation, and food.

Yosef graduated and broke my heart to take a job in the place that most spoke to his: Israel. He headed an international student activist organization that advocated for the release of Jews from Russia, Ethiopia, and Yemen. He was fasting in support of Jewish refuseniks in the Soviet Union. He was joining Israeli university students in protesting tuition increases. I was still in Cambridge, finished my master's degree in multicultural education—where I realized I knew nothing about being Jewish at all.

Chapter 8

Getting Jewy

I was working with at-risk teenagers at Farr Academy, a school for twelve- to eighteen-year-olds. They were mostly boys, and mostly violent kids who had been expelled from their public schools and needed a therapeutic environment. The staff at Farr Academy worked to give each teenager the tools to build a different kind of life from their families of origin—whose stories made my family's struggles look like a sitcom. The idea was to "break the cycle of _____." Fill in the blank: poverty, illiteracy, drug abuse, teen pregnancy, neglect. All of the above.

I wanted to be a good teacher and help them find their place to stand in the world, but, rudderless and anxious, I had not found mine. I didn't know how to teach these kids. I avoided my own sense of ineptitude by blindly, distractedly getting through each day. The directors and other staff whom I admired like crazy seemed to intuit life's inherent worthiness and that helping kids climb out of the muck was, in itself, noble. I knew it, too, but couldn't quite *believe* it. Was it enough to be upstanding, drug-free, home-owning, charity giving, educated? What was the purpose of the better life that my parents had achieved and for which we hoped for our students? Where would these kids—where would *I*—find real *meaning*? There had to be something beyond us, some sort of cosmo-glue that binds ideas to hearts, hearts to each other, one generation to the next, all of us to . . . to what? I didn't think about the word "holiness," but I did think about what I came to understand as its opposite: waste. Humor, compassion, and inquisitiveness sometimes sparked in the kids, but I never saw it in their parents. They sat slumped in meetings at school, looking at their fingernails or engaging their kids in side arguments that became the main focus of the meeting. *I told you not to lean your chair back. Sit right!* Again and again. It was like the kid in the chair and the parent had an understanding: Let's make the meeting about something we can handle. If I had had any skill I would have been able to turn the meeting around, but I sat dumb, glued to my notes, made helpless by the lack of light in (usually) the mother's eyes, the lack of connection to anything transcendent, to the possibility of transformation. The world had beaten her down.

It was one of those Friday afternoons at the end of another long week at Farr: a boy's violent eruption in the halls, a girl kicked out of her house with nowhere to go, an AWOL student who had been arrested for stabbing another teen on a subway platform. I was ready to join a silent monastery and be like Yentl, only a monk. Mentl? I shut myself in a school office and wearily changed into my skirt for Friday night services. On Friday afternoons, after the big weekly staff meetings, my coworkers went to a local bar to drink, shoot darts, and unwind. I enjoyed it but, weirdly, it was the campus Jewish center, Harvard Hillel, that beckoned me—and not just because my stepmother, Janice, had been encouraging me to get over Yosef, who was living in Israel, and meet a Harvard man.

It was a twenty-minute walk amid the turning fall leaves, and later the baring trees, and finally the dark, frigid winter, but off I went each week. At first I knew no one and sat at the back, engaged but tentative, in the Reform service. By the time spring came around again I had learned the prayers and songs by rote and had met new friends, mostly graduate students, and was regularly joining them for Shabbat dinner. And Shabbat lunch. Throughout that year, working in a tiny corner of a troubled world and praying in a Jewish setting moved alongside each other in my life, like films unspooling on separate reels. What I didn't realize was that it was all part of the same story, waiting to be spliced together.

Suddenly, in that tiny windowless office, wearing my Shabbat clothes and packing my work outfit into a bag, I thought: the Berrigan brothers. Abraham Joshua Heschel. Martin Luther King Jr. Anti-war, anti-racism activists all. All clergy who sought that connection between the immediate and the transcendent.

I'll become a rabbi.

I picked up the phone—a black wall phone with a round dial. Impulsively, I called information for the number of Hebrew Union College–Jewish Institute of Religion, a rabbinical school in New York City. It was the only rabbinical school I had heard of—a college friend of Yosef's had gone there.

"Hi, my name is Susan Silverman. May I please speak with the admissions officer?"

"He's gone for the day," said the receptionist in a curt tone.

"Okay, I'll call back tomorrow."

"*Tomorrow is the Sabbath*," she said with a godlike boom.

"Goddammit," I said under my breath.

Three months later I was accepted to rabbinical school. My father joined me one Friday night at Harvard Hillel, perhaps to see what all the fuss was about. After services, my new friends gathered around him. "*Mazel tov* on Susan's acceptance to rabbini-cal school!"

"A rabbi!" my dad exclaimed in impish glee. "We didn't even know she was Jewish!"

He waited for the laugh, then added: "When we found out, we sat *shiva!*"

I was as surprised as my father. I couldn't imagine actually be-coming a rabbi, not least because I didn't know what rabbis did, having almost never stepped foot inside a synagogue. But the idea held such possibility, and the first year of study would be in Israel, so I'd be with Yosef. "You'll make a wonderful rabbi," he said over one of those expensive international phone calls.

The reaction from everyone else I knew was worth the price of tuition: Silence on the other end of the line, and then, "*What did you say?*" Or blank stares. Most of the people I told froze, then laughed. Or, from a high school friend: "But you were class flirt!"

My first year of rabbinical school, in Jerusalem, I didn't even have a basic Jewish vocabulary or experience of the holidays. I muddled through my studies and in classic avoidance mode spent most of my time volunteering away from campus—co-leading an Arab-Jewish teen group and tutoring English in an Arab high school—or hanging out at Yosef's work, a place where I found comfort in being seen as his girlfriend even as we both lacked con-fidence in any future together. On my campus, I heard murmur-ings from other students about me. *What the hell is she doing here?* Mean, but understandable. I didn't even know the Hebrew alpha-bet. One time I tried to incorporate "Amazing Grace" into morn-ing services.

I was at a loss academically and in my relationship with Yosef. At the end of the school year we broke up. Again. Yosef would stay in Israel and I would return to the United States. As I settled into the taxi for the airport, Yosef played jack-in-the-box at the window, making me laugh even though I was sobbing. He headed to the local *mikveh* to mark the end of our relationship and start fresh. I sort of knew what a *mikveh* was.

The second year of the rabbinical program at Hebrew Union College–Jewish Institute of Religion was in New York. I took an apartment in the East Village with a band-manager roommate I found in the paper who referred to the place as a "den of iniquity." With her, I felt rabbinic. In that apartment, I was the top Talmudist. I led High Holiday services at a small congregation in upstate New York that hired a rabbinical student each year for Rosh Hashanah and Yom Kippur. I slogged my way through the Hebrew prayers, reading phonetically, with transliteration penciled above the long words. Notes in the margins of the extra-large prayer book I special-ordered read, again in my penciled handwriting, *Turn to ark. Bow. Turn back to congregation. Motion for congregation to sit. Turn to page 72 and read from top.*

My internship as student rabbi at the Columbia University Jewish Center began after the holidays. As at Farr Academy, I plodded through with no real skills or instincts for the work. The students were knowledgeable Jews, and I nodded as meaningfully as I could when they planned programs to which I would show up and muddle through again. I floated helplessly without Yosef in my life, without his sense of purpose on to which I could glom.

I finally broke down and called him. "Let's make it work," I said. He said he needed to think.

A few days later at the office, someone handed me a fax. "I have two tickets to Mexico over your winter break. Details to follow. I love you."

It was a Friday afternoon in spring and already hot. The metal fan batted paper towels and crumbs around the kitchen but left us sweaty as I chopped vegetables on the placemat-sized countertop of our rented sliver of a brownstone in Washington, D.C. The trip to Mexico three years earlier did its job and we were engaged.

"There's a meeting for prospective adoptive parents," I said.

"We're adopting *now?*" Yosef asked.

It was a sincere question. He wasn't trying to start an argument, but it wasn't a ready agreement, either. That was Yosef: game for anything, but also hard to engage because of all the other shiny activist things pulling him in every direction.

For many people this would not have been the time to start a family, adoptive or otherwise. We were planning our wedding for September. Yosef had a new job as an editor at a Jewish magazine, with a salary that would not begin to pay off his student loans. I was commuting to school in Manhattan during the week and to my student congregation in New Hampshire every other weekend and on Jewish holidays. A friend of ours had just been held up at gunpoint outside our house.

"Is this about Tyrone?" Yosef asked. A friend of ours, as part of his medical residency, was treating a severely diabetic four-year-old in the city's foster care system.

"Maybe," I said. "But let's start the process and see where it leads."

We went to the meeting. We listened to social workers talk about "waiting children"—the ones who are hard to place because of age, illness, psychological challenges, and any number of other factors. There were tables at the back with giant photo albums of children without families of their own—yet. We brought home a list of required documents and an application.

And then we discovered I was pregnant.

"I'm an unmarried, pregnant rabbi," I said happily as we hugged.

Yosef says that we were destined to be together, and you can't fight destiny. I say that our destinies are separate, but that we loved each other enough to claw, fight, and overcome our fates.

He says it figures that we can't even agree on agreeing.

On September 6, the sometimes vague, sometimes acute, chronic homesickness I lived with lightened as we gazed at one another beneath our tie-dyed silk *huppah*, our symbolic first home as a family. In the light of the candles our friends and family held in a circle around us, and in the glow of the deep, bold colors of the silk above us, the rabbi declared us married.

"Oh, shit," I said.

"It's okay," he said with a smile, and held out a tissue.

Chapter 9

Pre-Existing Condition

he pregnancy was neither planned nor unplanned. I told myself that being pregnant at our wedding was my last chance
to break the rules before conforming to marriage. And it calmed
me. It put my relationship with Yosef more firmly in the "permanent" column. We were becoming a family, period. My anxiety,
which traveled around my soul knocking on the doors to my heart,
stomach and mind, jumping up from behind thoughts, bursting in
on quiet moments, would have to find some other soft spot in my
psyche to crash through, like a crazed vaudeville performer through
a paper stage set.

By the end of the pregnancy I was seventy pounds heavier. That
is not a misprint. Yosef thought I was supposed to eat for three:
the fetus, the placenta, and me. He fed me accordingly. On April
26, 1993, as I plopped down on the couch to watch *Tootsie*—
cheese, veggie, and mayo sub in one hand, remote control in the
other—I felt a wetness. But I still had two weeks to go before my
due date! I should have known. At Thanksgiving, three months

into my pregnancy, Yosef's Grandpa Jerry—who communed with the unseen—suddenly announced at the table, "It's a girl and she'll be two weeks early," before returning to his mashed potatoes. The girl part was soon confirmed by ultrasound. The other part of Grandpa Jerry's prediction was now proving to be true as I sat draped in a wet, mayo-blotted muumuu.

Laura and Jody hopped trains from New York to D.C. I couldn't reach Sarah.

"You called your sisters before you called me?" Yosef said from his office.

"They have farther to travel."

He came home on the Metro, humming the song "My Girl."

Sarah had actually been on a flight from Los Angeles to New York for meetings with *Saturday Night Live*, where she had just been hired as a writer and performer, and had coincidentally been rerouted to D.C. because of a rainstorm. She called from a pay phone when she landed and got to the hospital before we did.

"Where's your luggage?" I asked as we hugged at hospital reception.

"I came straight here and didn't even go to baggage claim," she said. "I didn't want to miss anything."

She needn't have worried. Hours later I was berating her and everyone else who had arrived for the festivities, including my cousin Abby, for having the audacity to fall asleep in easy chairs or on the floor. I made them fetch me ice chips and popsicles and drugs. "Get me an epidural!" I screamed. Here I was, providing a daughter for my husband, a niece for my sisters, and a first-cousin-once-removed for Abby. It was the least they could do.

The actual delivery began the next afternoon. The doctor and nurses repeatedly asked my sisters and cousin to leave the room— just Yosef could stay—but they kept creeping back in until the hospital staff gave up. "Just stay out of the way," they said. The doctor was so good that even though she was crouched between my legs about to catch a baby, she noticed when Sarah turned sheet-white. Sounding like a commander in battle, and without taking her eyes off me, she pointed at Sarah behind her and said, "That one's goin' down." Laura caught Sarah right before she hit the floor.

And then came Aliza.

"I love you so much, even though I don't know what that means yet," I said to the skinny little thing with the wide face and a mop of black, brown, and blonde hair as I held her for the first time. I peered into her face the way the Israelites stared at the thunder and lightning of Sinai. I was entering a sacred covenant I didn't understand, and it filled me completely. From the first moments, I lost myself to the force of Aliza's demand on me, overpowered by love and awe. I had given life, but she gave it right back. I was someone new.

Laura would come home with us, but Jodyne had to get back to work at National Geographic and Sarah to *Saturday Night Live*. We left the hospital a few hours later, just before midnight, because our health insurance had found a way not to pay for the delivery—Yosef had switched jobs, and the new company called my pregnancy a "pre-existing condition"—and we could not afford an overnight stay. We got in the car only to realize that in our rush to the hospital, we had forgotten to install the baby seat. Laura sat in the back and held baby Aliza. But what if we have a car accident on the way home with the baby in Laura's arms and everyone dies? That felt inevitable, even as I agreed to the plan and buckled in.

That wasn't the only danger. We had left the hospital so fast that no one had taught me how to get a newborn to latch onto the breast. I couldn't get Aliza to nurse.

"She's going to die!" I cried.

When I was in fourth grade, my mother began driving me to Boston every week for our parallel therapy appointments. My sessions with Dr. Belfer were on the third floor. My mother's with Dr. Hauser were on the fifth. "Don't forget to come get me," I reminded her as she dropped me off at Dr. Belfer's office.

Experience has shown that the moment I relax my anxiety, something terrible happens. We went to stay at the beach for two weeks during the summer after fourth grade. For two blessed months I would never have to leave my mother's side, except for when she continued her weekly therapy sessions during our vacation. One week, after her session, she was going to go to the bus station in Boston to pick up Virginia Caret, a "Fresh Air" child who had already spent a few summers with us. Virginia was the epitome of cool. She was a year older than me, from Spanish Harlem in New York City, and wore tube tops, white hip-huggers, small gold hoop earrings, and a delicate gold chain with a crucifix. At home, she would stand in her bathing suit on the diving board of our backyard pool and sing Dusty Springfield songs in her Puerto Rican accent. *You don't have to say you love me, just be close at hand.* (I heard it as "just bring home a ham.")

Before my mother left, she asked my father to accompany her—she wasn't sure of the route from the beach. "Jesus, Beth Ann," he said. "It's my fucking vacation."

"I'll go with you, Mom," I said.

"No sweetie, stay at the beach. The Connors are coming today and you'll have so much fun."

Susan Connor was my best friend. My mother called us Twosie Susies because we were inseparable and looked alike: tall and skinny, with long, straight hair (mine brown, hers blonde), big eyes (mine brown, hers blue). But while I sought certainty in the love of the people around me, Susan found it in her devotion to God and Jesus, whom she loved more than anything. "More than your family?" I asked. "Even more than me?" was what I meant.

Torn, I shaded my eyes from the glare that bounced off the car as my mother started the engine. She had decorated her 1972 convertible with rough non-slip bathtub flower stickers and painted peace signs. As the "NOWAR" license plate and McGovern/Shriver bumper sticker disappeared in the distance, navigating the narrow Hampton Beach street between lines of parked cars, I relaxed. I couldn't go with her now even if I wanted to. Decision time was over and I could relax into the day of sand and ice cream and Monopoly with Susan, my sisters and Daddy, who, out of the presence of my mom, was a happy and funny guy.

On her way back to the beach that day, with Virginia in the passenger seat, my mother swerved—maybe glare blinded her for a moment, or maybe a car stopped short in front of her?—into oncoming traffic and crashed head-on into a car with four elderly women. Virginia, who was seat-buckled at my mother's insistence even though my mom had not buckled herself in, was miraculously unscathed, as were the four women in the other car. But my mother was taken to the hospital unconscious and bleeding.

When my father fetched Virginia from the hospital, Virginia brought back a shopping bag with my mother's clothing. Slowly and with macabre relish, Virginia reached into the bag and pulled out my mother's tennis shoes. Their new whiteness was spattered with blood like the Jackson Pollock paintings my mother had shown me in a magazine. "It's the motion that sets him apart," she had told me. "He can capture speed on canvas."

Virginia lowered the shoes gently, as if they had been made sentient by the human blood, and then removed my mother's khaki shorts and blue sleeveless button-down shirt. Blood had seeped into her clothes in large reddish-brown stains.

The only reason my mother lived through that was that my father made a pact with God. When he called from a pay phone that evening to see how she was, the nurse who answered put my father on hold while she checked on my mother. Waiting for what felt like a verdict, my father felt God say to him: "It's up to you. Will she live or die?"

He hesitated, but then whispered into the sticky receiver, "Let her live."

When I got home from the hospital after giving birth to Aliza and found that I didn't know how to nurse her, I cried and begged God to help. That was what had worked before. Then, early the next morning, I called my cousin Beth Jill, a neo-natal nurse who, thank God, lived nearby. Lighthearted and wise, she came over and taught me the basics of getting a baby to latch on. I followed her instructions step by step: pinch areola, bring baby close, tickle her lips with squeezed nipple. Soon it became natural. By the time Hallel came along twenty-two months later, I could nurse her in the crook of my arm while typing a sermon.

Yes, we went from zero to two children within two years. (Condoms, as it turns out, are not amulets that can protect you from their perch on the bedside table.) I now had two little beings to swallow me into that heart-pounding-like-God's-thunder-at-the-mountain love. Two daughters, Aliza and baby Hallel, to guard from death.

I felt like we lived our lives on Pac-Man routes. At any moment the muncher could round a corner and make one of us disappear.

Pac-Man or Psalm 23? Judaism might have engaged me in the world more meaningfully and offered deeper metaphors than the muncher. *The Lord is my Shepherd, I shall not want,* for example. But my first exploration of Judaism had been in rabbinical school where I started off not even knowing the Five Books of Moses. Being a rabbi was still a job to me, not yet a deeper way of life. The values, sure. But being Jewish was not a set of metaphors and stories in which I placed myself or with which I grappled. Jewish ways of being were the tools of my trade, but even though Yosef and I incorporated the rituals and values into our family, it didn't occur to me to really engage them in how I lived and oriented myself in the world. Had I been truly engaged in Judaism, I might have placed my painful sense of vulnerability among tradition's mothers: Hagar, whose son Ishmael nearly died in the desert but was saved when she saw a well. Rebecca, who saw an imminent threat to Jacob and sent him away in time. Leah, whose daughter encountered violence yet returned home whole.

To me, the traditional motifs were for sermons, not a basis for life. It was fodder for books, too, like the Jewish how-to I wrote with Yosef. It had a progressive bent, profiling multiracial, gay, and inter-married families. We hoped to illustrate, among other things, an organic relationship between Jewish life and progressive, activist values. With a four- and a two-year-old, I guess we were experts. And for the past few months, we had been taking turns traveling around the US, talking to groups in bookstores and Jewish community centers, and giving interviews on local TV and radio stations.

The one written text I always kept with me, the way others might carry the book of Psalms or a prayer book, was a worn sheet of paper, folded into thirds. It was a form letter. Black printed

words with blank lines to fill in—name, date of birth, marital status. Salary. Years of education. Criminal record.

To me, it was holy.

It was the Washington, D.C., Department of Social Services
adoption application from the meeting Yosef and I had attended.
As impersonal as it was, it was a symbol of my truest self. Through
it all—marriage, two daughters, three years—I had never removed
the adoption paperwork from my purse. My driver's license might
show my identity, but this form revealed my deepest self, and I began to see it as part of the constellation of the Jewish symbols, rituals and stories that composed, and deepened, our lives. Our family
life was ensconced in a Jewish world—Jewish school for the girls
and our weekly attendance at services. We played Jewish music (including Madonna, who Yosef pinned early on as having a Jewish
soul). But what does it mean to be a Jew if not bloodline? What was
the purpose of being Jewish? The nexus of Judaism, our family, and
a baby from perhaps another country created something new,
something that was beyond a bubble of habit, ritual, and comfortable, enclosed community. The paperwork pushed my Jewish identity outside the confines of our little world, and challenged me to
bring Judaism to my most passionate lifelong desire—adoption.

By the time Aliza and Hallel were five and three years old, re-
spectively, they were, as my sisters said, "very Jewy." So Jewy was
their little world that one December afternoon, as the four of us
drove down our street, Aliza pointed to a station wagon in the next
lane and asked, "Why is there a tree on top of that car?"

"This is the holiday when Christians put trees on their cars,"
Yosef told her. I took a hand off the steering wheel to gently slap
his arm. (Fast forward to the following summer, when Aliza saw a
car moving slowly beneath the weight of a sofa on its roof. "Is this
the holiday when Christians put couches on their cars?")

This Jewy-ness my kids inhabited so organically sometimes sent my sense of all that is normal into a tailspin. I grew up as one of four Jews in a New Hampshire high school of two thousand students, singing Christmas carols in our public school, mouthing "amen" to the pre–football game prayers "in the name of our Lord Jesus Christ." As far as I could tell there were two differences between Judaism and Christianity: One was the Christmas-Hanukkah divide, and the other was that Jews were Democrats and Christians were Republicans. That's pretty much how my school played out—1,996 Republicans and four Jews.

Aliza and Hallel were playing with the Barbie and Ken dolls they got for Hanukkah. It was my mother who had insisted, overruling my objections. When Aliza opened her gifts at her grandmother's house, she was awash in joy. "A Bawbie!" she whispered in astonishment when she viewed the contents of the first box. When she got to the package containing the brown-skinned doll in a gold sari, she burst out: "Jesus Chwist! Anothew Bawbie!"

"Do your dolls have names yet?" I asked, plopping down beside them.

"Rivka, Tzipora, Rafael, and Charlie," Aliza answered dutifully.

"*Charlie?*" asked Hallel, looking up at her big sister in disbelief. "Dat's a name?"

Oh, God, maybe I should introduce them to a non-Jew sometime.

The (mostly) biblical names of our children's dolls testified to our power as parents to define their world, while the dolls themselves testified to our limitations. Aliza had bestowed good Jewish names on the gods and goddesses of anorexia.

I held up one brown and one pale doll. "How about if Rivka and Tzipora get married?" I asked hopefully. A Jewish-identified, mixed-race, lesbian plastic couple will surely redeem my progressive ideals from Barbie's clutches.

"Tzipora's marrying Rafael and Rivka's marrying Charlie," Aliza corrected me.

"How about this?" I insisted. "Rafael and Charlie are in love. Look, they're holding hands." I pulled at their shapely plastic man-arms. "Rivka can be the rabbi who marries them," I added, mentally high-fiving myself.

The girls ignored me as they sorted out clothing, roles, and scraps of story lines. Hallel was carefully dressing them, holding up a shoe to Tzipora's foot and, with her crossed eyes, solemnly evaluating how it worked with the dress, as if she were concocting a test-tube mixture to save the planet. Hallel played with the dolls, but Aliza *was* saving the planet. She assigned superpowers to each one. My pale-skinned, brown-haired, bespectacled, kind of goofy, dance-y, exuberant child identified most with the graceful, sarong-clad Tzipora with a brown body and black hair, so she gave Tzipora all three powers—flight, breathing under water, and the ability to disappear.

Snow covered the porch outside the room's sliding glass door. I watched as the girls played, all of us snug inside our house with its turn-of-the-century innards clanking and wood floors squeaking. The warm lights of lamp and fireplace glowed against the cold, darkening days like emanations from a mystical source.

Watching the girls with their dolls, I imagined product placement for our next bookstore appearance—kosher gay Barbie dolls. Ken could wear a T-shirt that said "I HEART Matzo Balls" or "Circum-size Matters." Barbie could hold a sign that read, "Narrow but not straight."

Our Hanukkah menorah on the chest-high windowsill was Noah's ark, in which nine animals each had a place for a candle in its head. The little lion, set farthest to the right, had been broken and re-glued many times. On the final night of the holiday, with Aliza and Hallel standing on chairs, we placed a candle in it very gently. We lit the flames and sang: *Blessed are You, Eternal our God, Ruler of the universe, Who commands us to light the Hanukkah lights.* Then the four of us sat in the dining room to do one of the activities Yosef and I had written about in our book. We laid out four envelopes, each with a separate drawing on it. One was of a plate of food, one was a house, one had a sick-looking child, and the last one depicted the Earth floating between the moon and the stars.

We gave each girl eighteen one-dollar bills.

"Okay," I said, pointing to the envelopes. "This one is for buying food for people who are hungry. This one is to help build houses for people who need a place to live. This is to buy medicine for children in poor countries. And this is to help clean the air and the water on our planet. You need to choose how much money to put in each envelope."

"Well, you need food even if you're sick," Aliza said, pointing to the food envelope.

"But if you're sick, you can't eat," Hallel countered.

At a recent rally in D.C. she stood beside Yosef on the stage and was given a chance to address the crowd.

"But if you don't have a house you don't have a bed or medicine or a refrigerator," Aliza replied to Hallel.

The flames, like the Sabbath candles each week, leapt with the joy of potential, of co-creation with God. I imagined holding a small child in my arms, one from a faraway place, glowing in the flickering light, smiling at the sound of the girls' chirpy singsong. *Look, baby, see the candles? Aren't they pretty? Do you want a present?*

I looked at the girls in their matching *101 Dalmatians* pajama blankets, happy and dance-y, their curly brown and blonde hair newly cut below the ear, sparkly in the flames that stretched upward, little revelations of God's original light, illuminating a path to our re-created family.

The sweetness of their smiles and hugs, the joy they emanated, was almost too much to absorb.

I turned to Yosef. "It's time," I said.

Chapter 10

African Cradle

"*J* want to adopt from abroad," I told Yosef. "And I don't mean from a lady."

"Huh," Yosef said in a high voice, the onomatopoeia we had coined for the sound a thought makes when it bounces off the brain, rejected for lack of sense.

"I mean, I guess, ultimately, also from a woman."

The opposite of losing a child to an unreachable place is getting one from an almost-unreachable place. I was captivated by the closing of distance; the unlikely, world-spanning joining of mother and child; the beauty of two divergent paths becoming a family.

"What about domestic?" he asked. "I wonder if we are first obligated to give a home to children in our own backyard?"

"How do we define backyard?" I countered. "There's physical proximity, but also the ethics and ideals we care about. Another country might be far away, but it's close to our hearts. What place are we drawn to? What calls to us?"

We had moved to be close to our eight parents—the advantage of divorce and remarriage is extra grandparents for the kids. With that kind of love and support all close to Boston, we realized we'd be crazy not to move there. The car was packed and ready for our four-hour drive to New York for Thanksgiving with Yosef's mother's family. And now we were figuring out how to bring another lucky grandchild into the family. I had recently attended a huge adoption conference where, in one session, the presenter showed vibrant images of hungry, lonely-looking children from orphanages in Eastern Europe, Africa, Asia, and South and Central America, followed by slides of the same children happy and healthy with their new American parents. In the busy hallway between sessions, people compared notes and discussed upcoming workshops. I met a woman who had adopted two boys from Central America.

"How did you find them?" I asked. "What guided you to the right country and orphanage?" Where was the divine map to our destiny? How could we lift the veil of mystery so we could see?

"Each step has a clue from God," she said as if she were giving directions to the mall. "Every time you make a choice that feels right, you go with it and take the next step. If it doesn't feel right, you look for other options."

That's how Yosef and I decided to adopt a boy. It's not that we wanted a boy, per se; we just felt like our future child *was* a boy. Well, I did. Also, he would be different from his sisters just by being male. Maybe that would make less prominent other, possibly painful, differences—color, genes, maybe even (God forbid) sense of humor.

Late that afternoon, on Route 84 in Connecticut, the girls fell asleep and we could talk freely. The faces I had seen in a slideshow on international adoption swirled in my mind. I usually drove, but I asked Yosef to take the wheel. That way, he couldn't read the paper or do any work. I had him captive. Yosef was so busy and distracted in our daily lives and hard to pin down to move this process forward. He was ambivalent about having another child at a time of strained finances. Sometimes I would yell and cry—*I have put my career on hold so you can work the way you do, travel, build your dream. Adopting is a dream I can fulfill while I'm holding down the fort.*

The sky was darkening and Yosef turned on the headlights, brightening the white lane markings that guided us toward Yosef's crazy, bursting-with-love-and-randomly-into-song family. *The opening of Your word gives light, and grants understanding.*

"Okay," I said, "let's do it. Guatemala?" I held out a postcard from the conference picturing a brother and sister's faces.

"Doesn't call to me," Yosef said.

I was ready to fight, to make him engage. Was he resisting the process? Or did he really just know in his deepest Spidey-senses that Guatemala wasn't our place?

"Korea," I said.

"Again, no pull. I would like a country with a Jewish connection."

"Russia?" I asked. I was not personally pulled toward Russia, but I waited for his reply in this high-stakes car game.

"I think it's Ethiopia," he said.

Bingo! Yosef had been active in bringing Ethiopian Jews to Israel, and we had both been awed by the stories of these Jews since the time we were in college. "Yeah, me too," I said, recalling the four embroideries of biblical scenes that we had hung above the piano in our living room. Ethiopian Jewish artisans sewed brown-toned characters—Joseph in his colorful striped coat, Moses with his staff, Miriam dancing with her timbrel, and King Solomon on his throne welcoming the Queen of Sheba.

We followed our instincts, just as the stranger at the adoption conference had advised. There was no algorithm to lead me to "my" child. There was only one brave step at a time. And I loved the steps. I was disappointed in a way that we had come to the decision so quickly. I had Yosef engaged in a discussion about adoption, and I didn't want this little car-mission to be over. There was nothing else I wanted to talk about.

First thing after Thanksgiving I made a list of the adoption agencies that placed children from Ethiopia. I chose the second one I called. It felt right. African Cradle Adoption Agency was in Modesto, California, but worked with families from all over the country. Colleen, the office manager, answered the phone, and in moments she felt like a friend. She told me about Amber, the founding director, who was, herself, adopted from Ethiopia by an American couple when she was eleven years old, after she had lost both hands in a land-mine explosion. "We'll send you a big ol' packet of paperwork," Colleen told me. "It's mostly self-explanatory, but if you have questions I'm right here."

A manila envelope soon arrived stuffed with forms, lists of official documents we needed to gather (birth and marriage certificates, police background checks, fingerprints, criminal clearance), and also essay topics and forms for getting personal recommendations.

The adoption paperwork was tedious at times but always clear-cut, and therefore comforting, in contrast to parenting the live children already in my care. Life was so messy, with Yosef's work, the household whirlwind, the girls. Aliza was so grim for an almost-six-year-old. She played *The Phantom of the Opera* as the background to her bookish life: art-filled Japanese manga and hex-filled Harry Potter. Was she normal? I sometimes found her meticulously doing her Hogwarts homework. Which was funny, because the homework she managed to do for her brick-and-*mortal* school was stuffed, wrinkled, and un-turned-in at the bottom of her backpack.

Meanwhile, Hallel, four, was over-engaged in reality. She took everything personally, which fueled her violent streak. In a new twist, she had recently been biting her best friend just before lunch every day at preschool. With our mystery son, I could be a good parent just by neatly completing forms. Sharpened pencils, color-coded checklists, arrivals of documents in the mail and placement of them in three-ring binders.

The meetings with Rhea, the social worker from Jewish Family and Children's Services, were fun. We presented so well. The girls were basically on good behavior. The house was clean. Not that Rhea cared about those things (she didn't). The important thing was that we were good, loving parents, giving it a good shot, and in our meetings with Rhea we could remember that.

One rainy Wednesday, Rhea was coming over at four, after I picked up Hallel from preschool at 3:30. Dishes done, laundry put away, clutter disposed of, beds made, I still had a couple of hours until I had to pick up Hallel. Rhea said not to clean for her, and I believed her, but I enjoyed really going at it on her behalf—reaching in deep and removing the undercurrent of junk and clutter. I felt lighter, happier, abler. Yosef and Aliza were away on a father-daughter activist trip to a rally that Yosef had helped organize, to protest proposed congressional spending cuts in social services for indigent, elderly immigrants.

"Hold her hand tight in that crowd," I said to Yosef.

"We'll be on stage!" he replied.

I visualized a bulky white male in the crowd wearing a denim vest over a US flag T-shirt, pulling a gun and aiming it at the stage. "Please, just tell me you'll protect her!" They had, in fact, survived the rally where Aliza addressed the crowd. Yosef had prepared her with a line from the prophets: "Do not oppress the stranger, for once you were strangers in the land of Egypt." Instead, she improvised.

"You all come to my birthday party?" she blurted into the microphone, and ten thousand Russian and Latino immigrants, on the verge of losing health care and food assistance, laughed.

For Yosef, going away meant life. It meant securing rent and food for elderly immigrants while raising money for his nonprofit so we could pay our bills. For me it meant Yosef would die. I was horrid to him before he left on a trip, which was most weeks, and just as angry when he came home from one. I took it personally. If he went away, it was because he didn't love me enough. He was choosing fundraising meetings and conferences over me.

My loved ones could at any moment meet a horrible death, this was a reality of the world, and I allowed that terror to mold my behavior. Until he landed, I checked the news for word of a plane crash. Once, upon hearing of a crash in Russia, I actually figured out how he could have ended up on that flight, a scenario that included a wrong gate and an absentminded ticketing agent. I had recently spent half the night dialing and re-dialing the front desk of his hotel, asking the same clerk to put me through to his room. I had left messages, but what if he didn't check them? What if the red light on the hotel-room phone was out? What if he were lying dead in the gutter RIGHT NOW?

"When you get somewhere, you're supposed to call me!" I said when I finally reached him. "What is so complicated?"

"Sorry, honey. I had back-to-back meetings," he said when I finally paused for air.

"What's the rule?"

"Always call."

God created the world through poetic speech. I patrolled mine through vigilant bitchiness.

Yosef and Aliza were to land at 3 p.m. and come straight from the airport to the meeting with Rhea. With the time I had alone in the house before getting Hallel, I plunked myself on the family room floor and dumped out the big box of playmobiles. NPR chatter kept me company as I sorted the miniature world into categories: people, animals, trees, tiny flowers, building materials, furniture, clothing. The sense of control was a drug, both calming and full of possibility. When everything was sorted into Tupperware and ziplock bags, I checked my watch.

Oh no.

It was 3:16 p.m., and we lived a fifteen-minute drive to Hallel's day care. I was late to pick up a kid I already had.

The school charged a dollar a minute for late pick-ups, but the worst part was the (understandable) look I'd get from the director. I had done this before, kept the staff hostage with Hallel until I waltzed in.

I dashed into the class for the three- and four-year-olds and rushed toward where Hallel was buttoning her sweater. Oddly, she ran away, peering over her shoulder now and again to make sure she was at a safe distance.

"Sweetie, come on! Let's go home," I panted. It was now 3:38 p.m., eight minutes late. Eight dollars. My sweater was itchy around my neck. "Stop, honey. Please, let's get your coat."

She screamed and ran into her teacher's arms. Suddenly I heard crying words from behind me. "Mama! Mama! Stop, Mama!" The words took shape in my mind, and I whirled around to find my daughter.

Hallel's face was red and wet.

I looked at the little girl in the teacher's arms—it was pale, curly-haired Jordan. I turned to Hallel and fell to my knees. We had been an absurd, frantic train—Hallel chasiing me chasing Jordan who had been running in fear.

"Oh Halleli, baby, I'm so sorry. I thought Jordan was you. Isn't that funny?"

She punched my chest with her little fist before she fell into my arms.

I looked up at the teachers (*did they look smug?*) and whispered, "Any biting today?"

"No," they laughed. They were round Russian women, and so loving. I felt bad for having made them out to be judgmental bitches while I was watching the minutes click past 3:30 on the digital clock in my minivan. "If we give her a snack, she doesn't bite." Or if I fed her an actual breakfast, I thought, and not a granola bar in the car. After she had spent a recent school night at a friend's house, she said, "It was weird. They eat breakfast at home."

I scooped up my sagging girl, worn out from a long day and a hard cry. I enjoyed the trusting weight of her body, her head on my shoulder. As we made our way to the main door the director nabbed me. "Do you have a minute?" she asked.

"I'm sorry but I'm in a rush," I said. "Did you know we're adopting a child from Ethiopia? The social worker is coming over at 4. I need to run."

She looked me up and down as if I were Exhibit A. "Maybe now's not the best time," she said, no doubt taking in my tight smile, Hallel's tear-streaked face, my coat pulled half off and my pocketbook dragging behind me.

We made it home at 4:02, just as Rhea was also pulling in. I was never nervous around Rhea. Answering her questions made me feel like a good mom looking at the expanse of our life and the rivers of love and wisdom that ran through it, even if there were hard, dry patches here and there.

"We've been racing around a bit," I said to Rhea, who caught up with me and with the tired, angry girl in my arms.

"Take your time," Rhea said. "Can I carry something in for you?"

I looked down our driveway for the taxi bringing Yosef and Aliza home. Why weren't they back yet?

My heart was racing at the image of a truck careening into them on the highway. The knock of police on our door. Rhea there to ease Hallel and me into our newly bereft lives. Could I still adopt?

I set out a plate of cookies. Hallel helpfully scooped spoonfuls of sugar all over it. "They'll be here any minute," I told Rhea, not believing it for a second.

When Yosef and Aliza finally walked through the door, I could exhale. Aliza came bounding in and launched into the cookies "Hi, sweet girl!" I said. "Um, Yosef? Rhea's here," I said pointedly. "She's been here *quite a while*."

Yosef was on his way up the stairs. "Just let me change out of my costume," he said. "Costume" was what the girls called his suit and tie.

This was our third meeting, and Rhea, thank God, was sincere when she said she was not looking for perfection. She just wanted to make sure we were sane and capable and loving, that we had the emotional and basic financial wherewithal to raise another child. She wrote in her notebook as we answered questions about our childhoods, our parents and siblings, our educations (sixteen years of higher education between us), our work, how we met, why we wanted to be parents, why we wanted to adopt. As we answered, my frustration with Yosef's lateness eased. We saw ourselves through Rhea's eyes—flawed, but plenty good enough.

Telling our stories to her at the end of a stressful twenty-four hours, Yosef and I were able to define ourselves anew: what we loved about each other, how we were raised and how we tried to raise our children, what we valued and cherished and hoped for. Rhea gave us the opportunity to reframe our lives into a narrative of blessing and possibility, and to remember that even in our muddling through, there were moments of clarity that felt like redemption.

Chapter 11

The Cosmos and My Bic Pen

*T*he quiet of nighttime. The girls are asleep and I can sit beside them in silence, feeling in sync with their *neshamot*, souls. *Elohai neshama she'natata bee, tehora hee.* My God, the soul you gave me is pure.

Aliza slept as she had since birth, on her back with her arms straight up at her ears. Her hair was still damp and sweet from grape-scented shampoo. I kissed her soft, dimpled fingers, recalling a story her teacher had told me that afternoon. Aliza had stood in the middle of a game the kids were playing and held up her hands, like a traffic cop. "Hey, stop!" she said loudly. The other children stared as Aliza turned to Debbie, a severely hearing-impaired child who often sat on the sidelines, and reached out her hand. "Come, it's your turn now."

I kissed my girl's cheek and whispered how much I loved her.

Then I perched on the edge of the bed where Hallel was sprawled. She had tossed and turned in her sleep ever since she could move independently—side, back, tummy—mumbling as she moved. What was she dreaming? She was a child of cheek-squeezing love (she squeezed *our* cheeks) and stubborn rage, who had, in her younger years, shown cannibalistic tendencies.

"I love you like crazy-cakes, my funny, kind-of-scary girl," I whispered to my now four-year-old, still fierce but no-longer-chomping-on-children child. "May you always be safe, healthy, and well fed. *You mine fo-eva.*"

My girls were safe and cozy in the soft cotton sheets my mother had bought them. ("Honey, never buy the girls sheets with fewer than a 250-thread count.") My mother was always so clear about what we needed. She gave us things I didn't ever consider until we had them. Extra-soft sheets for the kids. Wrinkle-free travel clothes for Yosef. A loofah sponge for me. It really did soften the hard, dry bottoms of my feet. Our light-brown duvet cover smelled like vanilla because my mother had put a small net bag of scented gels in the wooden trunk at the end of our bed, "to give your sheets a slight scent of vanilla essence, like the scented oil you like."

"How come you've never noticed the vanilla?" I asked Yosef as I held the blanket to my face.

It was as if my mother had an Excel spreadsheet of what her children needed and when, from birth to death. "Oh, I guess when you're thirty-three-and-a-half you'll have to loofah the bottoms of your feet in the shower." She kept me apace with what she per-ceived as the demands of my age. Someday, when I'm old, I'll get a letter from her executor with a bottle of Nivea hand cream with age-spot remover with a letter telling me how I should dry my hands before applying it. *Not wet, so that the cream dissolves, but damp so it traps the moisture.* And she will be right.

She knew what words I needed, too. As she dried the newly rinsed set of unbreakable wine goblets from Costco, I said, "What if I don't love an adopted child like I love the girls?"

She laid the dishtowel across the glasses that sparkled upside down, and said, "When that child looks up at you and you realize that you're it for that kid, that the buck stops with you, the love will just be there."

It's a practical thing, love. My family appeared shambolic, but love oozed through our many cracks, through our messy attempts to know, to understand, one another. But what happens to a little boy's thoughts when he has no one who shares them? What happens to a little girl's memories when they haunt her? Do these memories get caught in the throat? Burn behind the eyes?

The unknown-ness of each child in an orphanage—or on the streets or worse—the memories, passions, joys, fears, struggles, and what makes them laugh, all of it must increase a lonely sense of being indistinguishable from the child in the next bed as they are squeezed into shapes by necessity.

We are all broken, we just are. But if we are a little lucky, and very willing to learn how, our shards and pieces can form mosaics of love and relationship—unwieldy, vibrant, and cracked as they must be. If we are not so blessed, we need to fit to whatever form is known or available to us. Kids in institutions or making their way on the streets take on outer shells of conformity and necessity.

A splay of glow stars sparkled above the girls as they slept. Standing on a ladder with her neck bent back and arms raised, Laura had painstakingly organized the stars by constellation. When she tired of following the chart that came in the box, she scattered the rest of them across the white ceiling. I was happy not to have them ordered just so. I'm not interested in finding these forms in the real sky. A belt? A dog? For me, the stars are questions, not answers. Possibility, not defined figures. The heavens declare the glory of God. The firmament shows God's handiwork, says the psalmist.

For the sake of our child-to-be, Yosef and I would navigate forms, interviews, regulations, bureaucracy, heartbreak, and hope—swinging from star to star—to the other side, where a child will lovingly be tucked in, sung to, and kissed goodnight, just as every child deserves. And when this child grows up and has children I'll make sure they sleep in sheets of the softest cotton.

"You're mine forever" was a family mantra. My sisters and I even used it as an abbreviated email sign-off to each other: YM4E.

Here is how it came about.

It originated with Hallel when she balked, as only a three-year-old can, from parting with her best friend, Clara, after a long day of playing together.

"I'm not leaving!" Clara yelled, matching Hallel's passion, as her mother held out a small red wool coat with white faux-fur trim. Sitting on the floor, Hallel and Clara clutched each other with their arms and legs.

"Impressive," Yosef said with a smile, proud of Hallel's political resistance technique. "If they hold their limbs inside the huddle they'll confuse the police dogs."

Yosef held our tenacious girl around the waist as Clara's mother extracted Clara from the little girls' tight embrace. Hallel's face was smeared with tears and her feet were ready to sprint. Seeing any separation slaughters me, even one as non-traumatic as two very loved little girls who must part for the span of a night's sleep in their sweet beds. I barely refrained from suggesting that Clara spend the night, as Aliza, two years older than her despairing sister, loosened Yosef's grip on Hallel one finger at a time, her lips pursed determinedly between her wide cheeks. She was my daughter all right, fighting separation between loved ones with all her might, just in case the simple act of parting gave God a nefarious idea.

Now free from her father's grasp, Hallel lunged for the door and yanked it open. In the short distance, beyond a few deep boot prints in the snow, Clara called over her mother's shoulder, *Bring me back!* A whoosh of Boston's December cold stopped Hallel just inside the threshold. Her black velvet dress shimmered in the wind, her thick red tights rippled around her knees, her pink-rimmed glasses were askew, and her blue eyes, the strabismus yet to be surgically adjusted, stared vehemently at each other. I crouched beside her and wiped her hair from her face. I tried to bring her close to me, to hug and kiss and comfort her determined little self, even as I knew, and told myself repeatedly, there really was nothing sad here. But my rational mind was no match for my gut instinct: any tears of good-bye had, at their source, death—the possibility of a loved one disappearing, leaving a hole that, unlike Wile E. Coyote's body shape in a brick wall, had no one size or set of contours. Any talk of good-bye summoned this empty space like an odorless, nauseating gas.

Hallel resisted my embrace and leaned toward the cold. *"YOU. MINE. FO-EVA!"* she wailed into the black night.

Forever was a big deal to me. "No dying" was my rule to Yosef who, under duress, would promise me that he and the kids would not do so.

It was in that winter of the YM4E talisman that we began our (well, my) long-awaited adoption process. By that cold, declarative night, I had been browsing literature, checking websites, and looking at photo listings of waiting children. It was like being pregnant while all the babies that could ever be conceived float around you. Which one will pop out at the end?

Mostly I perused the adoption magazines that I kept on the bedside table. The captions below the photographs read, *We Help*

Make Families. He's Waiting for You. Does She Have a Place in Your Heart? My stack of novels lay untouched because I was taken in by the perversely addictive combination of pain and possibility advertised in orphans' eyes.

"Look at these faces," I said, interrupting Yosef's bedtime reading. I held a magazine open to a picture of six wide-eyed Chinese toddlers in a row of high chairs. "I want them all to grow up knowing they're adored."

"They're sweet," Yosef admitted, "but the images stick in my mind. It's upsetting, and it doesn't really get us anywhere, honey. Let's focus on the paperwork for Ethiopia."

I knew the pictures well. The faces appeared to me in the halls at Hallel's day care and in shopping carts at the supermarket, the way you might think you see someone you know from afar hailing a taxi or in line at Starbucks. And I wanted Yosef to immerse himself in this world with me. Even though he was right. There were no answers for us in these magazines. They were destined for the recycle bin. I could fantasize about making a home for thousands of children or actually make a home for one. No more whispering "You mine forever" to faces from Guatemala and China and Russia. No more vain fantasies.

"Okay, let's look at the paperwork from the agency," I said.

I picked up the manila envelope we had received from an adoption agency, and Yosef put down his newspaper. I hadn't opened it yet, hadn't yet been willing to abandon the fantasy and enter some ass-kicking reality: Once the forms were complete, our file would join hundreds of others on the desk of a bureaucratic matchmaker—a faraway woman at a desk, surrounded by stuffed manila folders or clear plastic sleeves in binders. Half the files would be filled with information on prospective parents like us. The other half with photographs, biographies, and medical records of children. *For Papa, make him a scholar! For Mama, make him rich as a king!*

Maybe Xue the Matchmaker sits in an old Soviet-style office building in Beijing sipping bubble tea, and Sunita the Matchmaker drinks *lassi* in a Gothic structure in Mumbai, and Mio the Matchmaker sits in Hong Kong sipping *yuanyang*, and Yihune the Matchmaker savors muddy coffee in Addis Ababa, and Regina the Matchmaker tosses back a shot of Russian vodka. And maybe Xue's bubble tea spills on one of the two piles of forms, and in cleaning up the spill she puts the top document on the windowsill to dry, and staples the second document to the first document from the other pile, and instead of Mei Ling going to Esther Goldberg on the Upper West Side of Manhattan she goes to Erin and John O'Malley in Boston.

And maybe *that* was meant to be.

I rifled through the forms. Three stapled sections were held together by a paper clip. The pages were photocopies, black type on white paper, the text askew. I paused at the page of medical conditions, like the health history form you complete at a first doctor visit. But instead of checking off the ailments you had, you checked off the ones you were willing to have—in a child:

> HIV
> Clubfoot
> Blindness
> Deafness
> Cleft palate
> Spina bifida
> Hypospadias
> Hemangioma

Each mark, whether a "yes" or a "no," felt significant. Would a certain pattern of yes and no marks somehow lead us to our child? How could I divine these markers on our path, like constellations in a desert sky? And who was I to have this kind of power? God lifted the veil of creation, just a little smidge at the corner, for half a second, and showed me a glimpse of its inner workings. "Now," the still small voice said, "take a step toward your child."

I reviewed the column of blue Xs I had drawn. I had responded honestly, as honestly as possible. This was a partnership between my Bic pen and the cosmos.

I checked my last box.

Yosef pulled me close and stroked my hair. I stared at our bedroom wallpaper with its dense, Monet-like dots of soft blues, purples, and greens. The images shifted in my mind to become water, sky, grass, treetops, flowers. In the biblical story of creation God separated the lower waters from the upper waters to form the seas below and the sky above. The seas, now earth-bound, reached upward and wept, grieving over the loss of the heavenly realm above. "Woe to us," they cried, "for we were separated from our Creator!" A reunion would remain forever in the future, a tease on the far horizon. I knew that longing. I had seen it in the faces of children separated from the mothers and fathers who created them, with no horizon in sight. But soon I would wrap my arms around another child who, on the other side of the world, called out to a cold, unresponsive darkness.

For him, I would make our family an island in the vast, weeping waters of the world.

Chapter 12

The Purim Plan

The Rosh Hashana new moon blended into the surrounding blackness. I stared at it until I could discern that faint, round outline. Discernment was my heart's desire as we moved slowly toward identifying our child. The treetops, too, had disappeared in the night sky, but slowly the branches took shape.

Yosef and I took in the sky from the back porch, sitting beneath blankets on plastic chairs, holding hands and reflecting. Rosh Hashana is a time for reflection and discernment. I had patience for about three minutes of this. Blah blah blah listen better. Blah blah blah patience. Blah blah blah more time as a family.

Now let's talk about the adoption. I needed the fix.

We had access to the African Cradle website where we could browse photos, and I checked it obsessively. It gave new meaning to the term "children's catalogue." Instead of an inventory of clothes or toys for kids, it was an inventory of kids without new clothes or toys. Why not roll the dice and, whatever number we get, count so many photos in and that will be our child?

I worried about what was unknown. Yosef made use of what we had.

"How will we find our child?" I asked.

"We're naming him Adar, so we'll find him on Purim," Yosef said. Adar is the Hebrew month in which Purim falls, and in which Hallel was born. She would have been called Adar had she been a boy. Yosef said we'd be matched with our baby on Purim, in the Hebrew month of Adar.

"Our paperwork should be done around then," he said. "We have the name Adar, and it's a holiday about revealing what's hidden. Everything just seems to converge nicely."

I relaxed into the embrace of my Yosef's confidence like Lois Lane flying nestled in Superman's arms. Only back in time to sixth-century BCE Persia, to a beauty pageant to crown a new queen and to a decreed pogrom. A time of mass confusion—and Purim reflects that. It's a holiday that blurs distinctions. We wear costumes that make people harder to recognize. Everyone eats *hamentashen*, triangular pastries with a surprise filling. We drink (schnapps, Slivovitz) until we can no longer tell the good guy (Mordecai) from the bad (Haman).

The Purim story begins with Ahasuerus, the king of Persia, choosing a new wife. His only requirement was that she be hot, a veritable Persian pinup, so he held an Ancient Near East reality show, *Who Wants to Queen a King*? From all the lovely young ladies of the land he chose the loveliest: Esther, secretly a Jewess, who had been orphaned at a young age and adopted by her older cousin Mordecai.

Even as young Esther donned her crown, the duplicitous Haman sought to slaughter the Jews. He convinced the king, who was like an empty vessel to be filled by cruelty or kindness, that the Jews were a threat to Persia. This genocide was to take place on the eve of the full moon of the month of Adar. The date was decided by casting lots—the translation of which in Hebrew is *purim*, which became the name of the holiday, Purim. Esther knew she had to approach the king, admit her Jewishness and convince him to change the decree, but she was afraid. Her uncle insisted she go. *Mi yodea* ("Who knows?"). "Perhaps it was for just such a time that you became queen?"

"Who knows?" is not the most striking motivational message. No fortune-telling promises, no voice from a heavenly GPS (Godly Prophesying System?). It offered only a possibility. A simple question that in its quiet, practical way calls us to imagine possibilities and take risks for them.

Esther took a deep breath, approached the king, and revealed her true identity.

Esther, an adopted child, revealed her true self and brought redemption.

We, too, asked, "Who knows?" If we find courage to approach the unknown, we, too, might offer redemption. And, in turn, the revelation of an adopted child was the key to our own moment of redemption. But our son would not appear to us. We had to narrow the world down to him. On the adoption website, each child was a mask—a posed photo and some general descriptions. A computer click enlarged the photo and revealed bits of information: adorable, sweet, alert, loves to be held, enjoys other children. The descriptions pointed to sparks of holiness just waiting to be kindled by godlike American parents who would point, click, and maybe adopt. The power of adults over children is immense, a power like that of King Ahasuerus that can be used for magnificence or evil.

Who knows?

Still six months shy of Purim, I received a call from Colleen, the caseworker at African Cradle.

There was a boy. His name was Michael.

Just the day before, Yosef and I had discussed giving our new son the middle name Michael. It had been my baby brother Jeffrey's middle name.

"Susan, are you still there?" asked Colleen.

"How old?" I barely whispered.

"About three months. He was born on July 15."

My father's birthday.

"If you want him, he's yours," said Colleen. "I won't even put his picture on the website."

He's mine? I paced the narrow space between the two desks in our home office and finally fell into a chair. As a child I had watched my father pace, the phone tucked awkwardly between his ear and shoulder. He always looked trapped by the long squiggly phone cord tangling in on itself. I was cordless, yet unable to move as my heart drummed in sync with the wall clock. Adrenaline pulsed in my temples, my chest. The itchy pull of excitement—getting and sharing pictures, making travel plans, falling in love—tempted me toward taking this boy. But the still, small voice within me shone through what the adrenaline masked: This was not our time or our path. We had placed ourselves in a narrative—the larger Jewish story, metaphors, and yearly holiday cycle—that oriented us in the world. Grabbing at "signs" as they popped up—a name, a birthday—could make me crazy. They weren't part of a greater story, the complex, unfolding narrative we inhabited, developed and improvised.

That night, in the quiet house after the girls were asleep, I told Yosef over tea and cookies about Michael and all the flashing lights around him—the birthday, the name.

"Do you really want to pursue this child?" he asked.

"No. But what if the Purim idea doesn't happen? What if there is no child brought into the orphanage that day?"

I dipped a Milano in my tea. The outer layer of cookie absorbed the hot liquid, and I took a bite before it fell away.

A few weeks later, Michael was placed with a family in western Massachusetts, about an hour from us. "I'm happy and relieved he has a family, but I feel sad, too, like God spoke to me and I ignored it," I said.

"Or, you spoke and God listened," Yosef said as he scrubbed Hallel's head with baby shampoo.

I leaned against the sink in the steamy bathroom, imagining a birthday party treasure hunt with cute little messages from God sending us to the next stop. But what we had was practice, a way of living that guides us. *Emuna*, the Hebrew word for faith, had the same letters as the word for "practice"—whether for soccer or keeping kosher. We practiced the big stories that framed our messy lives, and sometimes in it all glimpses of truth sparkled.

"God talked to you?" Aliza asked, standing naked in the doorway.

We answered at the same time.

"No, honey," I laughed.

"Of course," Yosef said.

The girls, like all their friends, adored Purim. The kids dress up and put on makeup and eat yummy treats and giggle their way through parades and games.

Me? I hate it.

The chaos in the house: preparing the costumes, clothes strewn across the floor, smears of makeup on faces and mirrors, my nagging sense of failure as a mother of children who scavenge for costumes at the last minute. At the synagogue it's noisy and crowded, with too many sugary treats and drinks whose intake must be monitored.

This year was different. I had waited for Purim the way kids wait for Christmas, for a son the way kids wait for Santa—with wishful thinking masquerading as faith. I hoped that Yosef's intuitive planning came true, that our story would progress and a child would be made known to us.

The moon filled in with light, shining between the tangled branches at our window, and my yearning grew along with it. The moon will shine its light on a child, and he will be ours. In one of my earliest experiences of tradition really rooting within the recesses of my soul or psyche or whatever, the traditional blessing over a waxing moon filled my heart: *I dance toward you but cannot touch you.*

Now, counting down hours (three) and minutes (one hundred and eighty, or in Aliza terms six *Yu-Gi-Oh!* and Hallel terms six *Rugrats* episodes), I helped the girls with their costumes. After the evening's Purim party at synagogue, we would go on the orphanage website and find our son. Wouldn't we?

Yosef was on his way from Logan Airport and would, God willing, be home soon. My Nana lived in me, calling out "God willing!" in the back of my brain whenever there was an upcoming reunion with a loved one. But my dad also had a place in me, responding, "Hey, even if He's not willing, I'll be there!"

"Don't go," I had cried as usual before Yosef left on this trip.

"Sweetie, I have to. If I don't meet with foundations, we don't get money."

"If only I could know for sure that you won't die, that your plane won't crash, that you won't get hit by a car or mugged, or . . . "

"I'll be fine," he said firmly.

"You obviously can't know that. Nobody goes off to the airport and says, 'Bummer my plane's gonna crash.'"

We'd been going to therapy every other week. We reasoned that if we started while things were good in our marriage, we'd have a framework for when they weren't. Recently we had talked about how I needed to stop saying mean things.

"What should I do with the anger, then?" I asked our therapist.

"You're a grown-up," she said. "Deal with it."

This is me dealing with it: Yosef came home just as we were finishing up the costumes. He was wearing his costume—suit and tie—and as he went into our room to change clothes I said, "I have an idea. This Purim, why don't you pretend to be a husband and father?"

"I know it's hard when I go away, but stop it," he said.

The girls improvised outfits from the costume box and their closet. Yosef had given them a plastic makeup tray from CVS for just this purpose. "Oh great, more crap," I said when he brought it home. I hated that he was leaving on a trip, and I hated that we would need the tray because it would all be last-minute again. My kids would be parading next to friends who were in home-sewn, perfectly fitted cloth costumes. (And no, it was not because they had stay-at-home domesticated mothers. Their mothers were full-time doctors, social workers, financiers, way more accomplished than I.) My mother had sewn our Halloween costumes (when I was five, I was Batman, and my father was Robin), but I didn't inherit that particular bit of DNA.

With the makeup kit I had painted red circles on Aliza's wide cheeks that frequently expand into a smile so striking that even strangers comment on it with delight. This year she was a clown, wearing a red-and-yellow checkered one-piece suit with billowy sleeves and legs, and a curly red wig. As I was helping Hallel into her Peter Pan outfit, Aliza tapped me on the shoulder. I turned and screeched. She had added vampire fangs and was now either a scary clown or a very disturbing vampire. Unsettling as it was, I was more surprised at her choosing a straight-up clown costume. There were three things that disturbed her: clowns, live fish, and little pageant girls. I guessed that would rule out an Esther costume.

Hallel's green tights, pointy-collared green shirt and green boat-shaped hat no longer seemed like a costume, since she had been dressing like Peter Pan for some time, wearing these same clothes, clean or dirty, every day since late fall. She was Peter Pan–like: adult determination and focus, but on childish things. This was also a striking alter ego, because her brother-to-be was in a sort of Never-Never Land, and would come to us as if he had always been the very age he would be on the day we met.

Yosef quickly changed into his costume for the night. I harrumphed past him as he stood in the doorway of the girls' room in some sort of get-up. His face was scribbled in yellow makeup, and he wore a yellow T-shirt, his expanding belly falling over yellow swim trunks.

"Sexy," I said. "What are you supposed to be, anyway?"

"A jellybean."

At the synagogue party Hallel ran around with her friends, her round fists full of cookies and pretzels. Aliza watched from the side with a wry smile until her friend Miriam arrived and the two of them snuck off to a forbidden stairwell to enact Frodo and Gandalf, even though they were dressed as a vampire clown and Queen Esther.

I went to Yosef, and he kissed me on the forehead. I was grateful that even when I was a bitch, he never pushed me away.

"We'll find Adar tonight, right?" I asked. I would not let him off the hook. He owed me for going away. He owed me for promising that this was the day. It was time for him to prove himself. If he really loved me, we'd find our baby in just twenty-four hours.

When we got home, we helped the girls out of their costumes and into pajamas. With their hair damp and braided, they got into bed. I sat by them as they nodded off, and whispered my love into their fading consciousness, into their molecules.

The next night, as Purim came to a close (Jewish holidays go from evening to evening), Yosef and I went upstairs to our chaotic office. Amid the usual piles of papers and books surrounding the bulky tan computer monitors, I stood beside him, barely breathing, as he typed in African Cradle's URL.

No new child had been posted that day.

I slumped into a chair. "It didn't work," I wailed. Yosef's mantra is that if we think creatively, we can do anything. *Okay, buddy, start thinking.*

"Maybe Colleen is still in the office," he said.

I looked at my watch and subtracted three. It was not yet 6 p.m. in Modesto, California.

"Hi Colleen, it's Yosef, Susan's husband," he said into the phone. "I was wondering about available babies at the Children's Center. Right, uh-huh, uh-huh. Yes, we've seen their pictures."

My heart sank. Well, there was always Passover. We could contort the "birth of a people" story to fit our needs.

"Yes, thanks," he said. "But actually, we were wondering whether any child had been brought in today."

I started pacing again. Then I stopped in the doorway and touched the *mezuzah*, tracing my finger around the raised Hebrew letter "*shin*" that decorated it. *Shin* is the first letter of the *Shema* prayer, "Listen O Israel! Adonai is your God, Adonai is One."

Were we listening for something holy now? For God's will for our family? I wanted to meet Yosef's eyes, get a clue, but he was staring at the wall.

"Really?" Yosef said. He turned to look at me. "Today?"

I froze.

Holding the phone between his ear and shoulder, Yosef rummaged through the detritus on the desk for a working pen and usable paper. I thought I would burst. "No need to bother with that," he was saying. "Just send the pictures and the letter—he's our match."

A baby boy had been brought in that morning. He hadn't yet been processed, so he wasn't officially available, but he would be ours. We stood looking at each other as if under the *huppah* again, but with a canopy of fluorescent lighting, and instead of friends we were surrounded by paperwork, unopened bills, and unread articles. A daily reminder that for all that is accomplished, more remains undone.

"He was brought first to Missionaries of Charity, where he tested negative for HIV, and then, today, to African Cradle," Yosef said when he hung up the phone. "They think he's about three weeks old and they call him Daniel."

"Holy shit," I said.

"It's okay," Yosef reminded me.

Chapter 13

Our Dream

October 1999

*F*rom Addis Ababa to London, and now over the Atlantic to New York, almost everyone smiled at us. Maybe they were nervous smiles in response to my staring them down with my grin. I liked to think that together Adar and I represented something that made people happy, that transcended the two of us. He sat on my lap by the window and we watched morning break across the sky. The pink dawn rose like steam above the dark blue sea as if recalling the divine *kee tov*, "It is good," God's pronouncement on the formation of a new day. Like the dawn that was no longer night and not yet day, Adar and I were in the process of becoming. We were a weaving of opposites—tragedy and joy, mystery and intimacy. Perfection in all its fractured pieces, made in the image of God.

I had dressed him in the traditional Ethiopian outfit that Jody and I bought for him at *macala*, the outdoor market in Addis Ababa. The red tones of his brown skin deepened against the stark white cotton with hand stitching. His little bare feet were heart-burstingly soft against the bumpy blue embroidery at the hem of the pant legs, and the large four-petal blue and black flower embroidered on the shirt seemed to reflect the expansiveness in his huge dark eyes.

I had two larger outfits with the same design packed away for the girls. I couldn't wait to take pictures of my three children in their matching Ethiopian outfits with the embroidered starburst of a flower in the center of each shirt. I pictured them laughing together, the girls on either side of Adar, or standing in a row by size order, the Ethiopian garb embroidering their lives together.

"Excuse me," said an Ethiopian flight attendant. "Your son looks so beautiful in his traditional clothing."

"Thank you," I glowed. "I love the flower burst." I pointed to the stitching.

"Oh, that's very special," she said. "It's a traditional Ethiopian cross."

It seems the rabbi had bought her children the fall crucifix collection.

"Get me my bag," I whispered urgently to Jody.

As we began our descent to Kennedy Airport, the sky turned from pink to purple to blue, as if a rainbow were leaking into the atmosphere. When we exited through customs, Adar was dressed in a tie-dyed purple and blue onesie.

"I have never seen you change him so fast," Jody marveled. "It was like ripping the cloth off a table without moving a dish."

Sarah was jumping and waving from behind the waist-high metal barrier. The four of us hugged in a huddle. "Oh my God, oh my God, oh my God!" she gushed, looking into Adar's face. "Wow, Susie, I remember this outfit from when your girls were little, but he's gonna freeze." We pulled sweatpants and a sweatshirt out of the suitcase for him. Jody put fresh socks on his feet and kissed his cheeks.

"I'm your *pretty* auntie," Sarah said to Adar with a straight face.

"Hey, who's your *favorite* auntie?" said Jody. "Auntie Jody! When you get home, tell Auntie Laura and Auntie Sarah who your *favorite* auntie is!" And to me, deadpan: "Show him my picture every day. Or I'll kill you."

Jody was headed back to her West Village apartment in Manhattan. After ten days away, she needed to get back to work, but she was clearly much sadder to leave her new nephew than to leave me.

Sarah, Adar, and I flew the 45 minutes from New York to Boston. Home! But not the same home I had left the week before. It would be a new place, re-created by this boy on my lap, who was watching intently as his "pretty" aunt made raspberry noises on his bare foot.

"You know what babies love?" she asked earnestly, Adar's feet now nestled in her hands. "Ethnic jokes."

"And pooping," I said, as Adar let loose.

"Oh, *disgusting*," the woman behind us stage-whispered, and sprayed perfume in the air, which was worse than the diaper smell. How could she be disgusted by anything this boy did? Did not his, *our*, beauty overcome any imperfection? I changed him one last time before we went, finally, home together.

As we landed, I wondered how Yosef would react to meeting Adar. Would their first moment as father and son have a defining impact on their relationship? Maybe there's a good reason for infants having fuzzy eyesight—it's too much too soon to get an immediate sense of the people who will raise you.

Yosef has great instincts. The first thing he did when we met at the gate was to look at Adar and say, "Abba," Hebrew for Daddy, and start the kissing game. *Brilliant.* He and I kissed each other on the lips and then we both kissed Adar—one of us at each of his cheeks. It's a game we played with the girls, and Adar loved it. He smiled big amid the double-cheeked *mwah* kisses. As waves of airport travelers rushed past, our family formed anew.

At home, an excited crowd welcomed us. All four of my parents, my sister Laura, and the girls, who could barely contain their excitement. *Where is he? Where is he?* They squeaked in their tiny voices.

They greeted him with hugs and kisses and calls of Adari! Adari! Then Hallel became uncharacteristically silent as she stared into her brother's face. Suddenly she exclaimed, "I didn't know he'd have curly hair like me!"

"Can I hold him?" Aliza asked. Before I could hand Adar over, my father snatched him up.

"Oh what a lucky boy you are!" he gushed. "You don't have your father's eyesight or your mother's singing voice!"

"Donald," my mother cautioned. "Everyone, give them some space."

Laura and I caught each other's eye and smiled. Even though she lived in Los Angeles, Laura spent a lot of time at our house. She voiced a character on the animated television series *Dr. Katz, Professional Therapist*, which was produced in Boston. They flew her in for a week every month. I felt like the real beneficiary of that deal.

We went to the living room and sat Adar in front of the fireplace. Everyone gathered around him except John. He knew, as we did, that like all children Adar would eventually make his way to John's solid, loving arms.

The girls, wearing matching calico dresses, performed a song and dance they had made up. Then it was Adar's turn to perform.

We watched him crab-crawl—legs straight, palms flat on the floor. We repeated his names to him: "Dani, Adar, Dani, Adar." Janice was on all fours, looking into his face. "He's even mo-ah go-juss than his pictures!" The girls could not stop touching him, kissing him, and cooing at him. He seemed to love it.

Aliza clasped her hands to her cheeks and said, "This is our DREAM!"

It *was* our dream. It had certainly been my dream since I was a child her age.

At lunch, we placed Adar in a booster seat that attached to the table. Parents, sisters, and grandparents jockeyed to be near him. In Ethiopia I had stocked up on the food items Fitsum listed for me and traveled home with produce in my luggage. I knew no one at customs would stop us—we were too beautiful to suspect. In the hotel and then on the flight I had followed the regimen to the ounce every day, even calculating the meal hours against time changes as we flew. Now at lunch I demanded strict adherence to this menu.

I unpacked the Ethiopian rice cereal, applesauce, and very ripe bananas.

"Susie, it's okay. You can vary it a little," my mom said.

I would not be moved. It felt like a betrayal to Fitsum.

"He can't have American bananas?" asked Janice, looking at my mom in collusion.

Adar had his eyebrows raised, an expression he made when he was confused or concerned. Aliza looked straight into his face, her expression serious. Slowly and clearly she said, "Danee, Danee," as if trying to make him feel recognized.

A few days later, we began our reconfigured life in earnest. I had pictures from the trip printed and framed: Adar in close-up, Adar and me, Adar and Jodyne, and, front and center on our living room wall, Adar and Fitsum. We would not forget her.

I dressed Adar in some of the new clothes from my mom—a red turtleneck shirt, blue corduroy pants, and a yellow-cabled pullover sweater. His fire engine sneakers had red blinking lights. I searched my mind for anything we might need from the supermarket despite a refrigerator full of leftovers so I'd have an excuse to make an appearance with Adar. We owed the public a viewing.

Sitting on the pull-down metal seat in the grocery cart, Adar moved his little body to the supermarket's piped-in oldies station. I looked more at people's facial expressions than at the shelves. A Latina woman walked by and saw Adar dancing on his tush. She smiled knowingly and said, "I'll bet his father likes to dance."

"The *hora*," I thought wryly.

Adar and I pointed to mystery. We were a mother and son super team: Bringing joy in a magic bullet! Power of love like a locomotive! Uprooting assumptions in a single bound! It's a babysitter! It's an interracially married woman and her baby! It's adoption! What varied stories I imagined I represented in the eyes of others.

Later that afternoon I visited a college friend who was recovering from minor surgery. My assignment was to bring over her medicine—a venti vanilla latte. Arriving in the town center, I parked my minivan. I couldn't find the Starbucks. A wave of self-consciousness went through me: minivan, suburb, middle class. I was embarrassed to ask for directions to Starbucks because I felt like a caricature of, um, *myself*. As I released the car-seat buckle and pulled Adar into my arms, the inhibition became exhibition. With Adar in my arms, I could ask for the local Tiffany's! I was now something new, deep and complex.

I asked a woman who happily pointed the way. Reaching for the door handle, my mind fixed on a triple venti soy latte for myself, I caught Adar's and my reflection in the glass. So pure, this boy, and I had made him into a prop. I was using him to "pass" in my own distorted way. The shard of my egotism had already scratched the shiny new world of our family.

Driving home, I checked on Adar through the rearview mirror whenever I could. Snug in his car seat, he stared out the window at the stream of red brake lights. The autumn sun lowered behind the trees to my left, casting a red and orange glow. The rainbow that greeted Noah after the flood promised a future without more devastating waters. This luminous sky was not stark like a rainbow. Its color was seeping, spilling, sinking, turning to black. On our right a round moon was emerging—a shimmery, silvery white.

Sometimes the same moment holds both day and night.

Chapter 14

Jew-Making

J was so proud: My six-year-old daughter was transgressive.
Aliza was wearing an undergarment called a *tallit katan*, "little
tallit," under her clothes the way many religious men do in obser-
vation of the biblical commandment *You shall make yourself a
twisted thread.* Read it as you will.

The fringes at the four corners of the garment, called *tzitzit*,
remind the wearer to observe God's laws and of the Exodus from
Egypt—a story of transgression, liberation, purpose, and loss. Aliza had worn the garment daily for over a year, ever since we spent
a summer in Israel. Her *tzitzit* bounced at her sides, out from under her short calico dress. Sometimes Adar, in imitation of Yosef
during prayer, pointed and said, "kiss!" Aliza happily obliged,
touching the fringes to Adar's lips.

"Wow, honey," I told her. "You've worn *tzitzit* a long time
now. How come?"

"So I can remember what I want God to do," she said.

"Do you mean, so you can remember what God wants *you* to do?"

She was quiet for a moment. "That too."

Keeping kosher makes me think about how I use animals and nature. The Sabbath reminds me that my work and I are not one and the same. Some traditions don't remind me of any particular value, but I practice them anyway. Not wearing a combination of wool and linen? Fine, I'll do it because it helps me locate myself as part of the "we" of the Jewish people.

But, like my daughter, there are things I want to remind God to do. The Jewish relationship with God is not a one-way street. Our codified texts include instances of our ancestors challenging, defying and even laughing at God—to God's approval. Abraham challenged God not to destroy the innocent people in Gomorrah. Moses calmed God's fury and saved the Israelites after they built a Golden Calf at the base of Mount Sinai.

I challenge, defy, and sometimes even laugh about traditions that I believe undermine instead of affirm life. How do you show the world that you're a Jew? *Tzitzit*, yes. Challenging tradition, yes. Making one's own place within it, also yes. All of the above? My daughter rocks! The word for a Hebrew person, in Hebrew, is *ivri*—"one who crosses over."

To join our family and become a suburban Jew in the United States, Adar too traversed many strata—genealogical, geographical, economic, cultural. He made the journey, but we had to complete it, at least in the religious sense.

And although our family was liberal, I wanted an Orthodox conversion for our son.

"We should do it in a way that makes sense in *our* lives," Yosef objected. "We are authentic Jews who do not need Orthodox approval."

I agreed. But to me, this wasn't about how we viewed ourselves. It was about how others viewed us, because their opinions would have an impact on Adar. Orthodox Jews, for the most part, do not recognize conversions presided over by non-Orthodox rabbis. People who make God in their own image have a hard time seeing the Holy One in others, even though it seemed to me that a fixed view of God is the opposite of the One who appeared to Moses as fire in motion, something that would cease if contained. A limited view of God is dangerous. If you were an alien who landed in the US, you might gather that white men are made more completely in the image of God than anyone else. When we "know" who is superior or inferior, who is more or less godlike, of whom He approves and doesn't, then we have a limited God, one that is shaped into the image of the controlling few.

A hardened view of God borders on idolatry. Fixing an image in your mind is not so far from holding one in your hands.

Some Orthodox establishments are so self-righteous they even denounce each other's legitimacy. Ultra-Orthodox rabbinic judges in Israel have voided Orthodox conversions around the world, a political power play to discredit other rabbinic institutions and take greater power for themselves. Hundreds of Jews-by-choice who were converted by Modern Orthodox rabbinic courts woke up one day to find that they and their children had been ruled not-Jewish by Haredi rabbinic courts. If I were one of those Jews, I would have responded with a resounding, *Whatever.* They can say what they want, but I know who I am. Still, what if they tried to do something like that to my son? How would he feel? How traumatic would it be for him to have his mother in jail after grabbing a black-hatted rabbi by the side curls and slamming his head into a wall?

The Boston *beit din,* the local rabbinical court, was widely accepted among other Orthodox communities, and among all progressive communities who did not proclaim themselves the sole arbiters of Jewish status. I figured that if the Boston *beit din* performed the conversion, no one would ever cast doubt on Adar's bona fides.

How anyone could doubt our boy's place as a Jew was beyond me. Home with us only a few months, he was already raising his arms, signaling to be lifted, so he could touch the *mezuzah*, a small vessel in a doorway that holds a sacred scroll. He would touch it and then kiss his own little fingers. I usually forgot to kiss the *mezuzah* when I entered and exited a room, but now I took his hand and kissed his fingers after he did. A sacred chain.

Written on the *mezuzah*'s scroll are biblical texts: *God is one. We shall love God and keep the commandments.* Kissing it is a religious act, a Jew's affirmation of the sacred covenant. It was already a reflex for Adari before he understood it as an act of devotion or, rather, an act of devotion to God. Perhaps it was his act of devotion to us, a habit in response to our smiles. Isn't God's oneness affirmed in the unity of parent and child looking lovingly at each other? It's a unity like the one that shines in the picture on my desk. In the photograph, Adar stands on a chair next to Yosef, who is wearing his *tallit* (prayer shawl) and *t'fillin* (the translation is "phylacteries," but if you don't know what *t'fillin* are, you won't know what this is either). It's a close-up and there is a brilliant blue sky and the tips of trees behind them. Yosef leans into his son and holds the fringes of the *tallit* at Adar's lips. Adar's hair sticks straight up in a thousand coils above his round face, his dimpled hands holding Yosef's fingers, his lips puckered against the *tzitzit*.

Kissing the fringes of a *tallit* and kissing a *mezuzah* are not universal religious acts, like praying or giving charity. It's a very specific Jewish ritual, one among many that we began to weave into

Adar's life. Kissing—*tzitzit, mezuzah*, each other—is woven into the same cloth.

It is not a given that adopted children will be immersed in their new family's culture. There is passionate debate on this topic in adoption circles. Some parents give the birth culture a primary place in the child's life: culture camps, holiday celebrations, foods, language acquisition. Girls whose last names are Rosenbaum and Goldblum are schlepped twice a week to Mandarin class, although we never even considered a class in Amharic for Adar. At an adoption workshop for Jewish families I led in a local synagogue, there were two moms—a lesbian couple that had been married by the synagogue rabbi—with an adopted daughter from Guatemala. Like so many parents of children adopted from another country and culture, they struggled with how to make room in their daughter's life for her birth origins: "We're thinking about raising our daughter with Mayan traditions and beliefs," one of them told me.

I realized that I had it easy. Ethiopia has a Jewish subculture, and for us to celebrate Sigd—the Ethiopian Jewish celebration of Jerusalem and Torah—was consistent with our lives. To have a kosher Ethiopian meal, wear white on Shabbat, have Ethiopian Israeli Jews in our lives—all natural and easy. These moms had less-fluid options. Mayan culture did not flow into Judaism; they had to dig a stream, and I was suddenly weary. How does one pass on something they don't have at all in their lives, that's not theirs to "give"? And, at the time, I had little patience for any hint of "DNA is destiny." It was used by the anti-international-adoption forces that infuriated me—that insisted children live in institutions or on the streets (or in millions of cases, trafficked) in their birth countries rather than with permanent, loving families abroad. "You can't rob a child of her/his culture." That attitude is why God wanted us to show up at Sinai early, before we fully woke up. Even the sacred can be objectified and used as tools for our personal purposes.

"If she was born to American social conservatives, would you raise her as a Republican?" I asked, immediately regretting my snarkiness. To my relief, they laughed.

We can only give our children what we have to give. The stories we tell them become who they, and who we, are. Yosef and I also, of course, had to just make our best guess, and we tried to give Adar a multilayered place to stand among the "we" of the Jewish people. Even, or especially, including gaps left by a lost birth culture. Desperately trying to fill those gaps, we believed, would only shut out the light that filtered through.

And Adar took to Jewy-ness. He kissed the *mezuzah*, said Hebrew blessings, waved his dimpled hands over the Friday night candles. A fluttery thrill of transgression waved through me because our lives were made via wormhole—the theory in physics that there are distortions of space and time that link faraway parts of the universe to each other. Adar had been transformed and transmitted via a social wormhole into our family and a Jewish universe. A world with gaps that he would just have to live with, that we wouldn't go crazy trying to fill. We could acknowledge, experiment, taste—sometimes literally. I made vegetarian Ethiopian sauces and bought *injera*, the spongy bread. We added to the Ethiopian Jewish art in our house. We traveled to New York City for a huge Sigd festival, the Ethiopian Jewish celebration of receiving the Torah at Sinai, held at the Manhattan JCC, a large Manhattan Jewish community center.

When it came time to arrange for Adar's conversion, I picked up the phone and dialed.

"This is Rabbi X," said the voice on the other end of the line.
"What is it we can do for you?"

I noticed his use of the royal "we."

I told him that I was an acquaintance of his colleague, Rabbi Y,
who recommended I call because I had a one-year-old who had
come home from Ethiopia a few months ago. Next week he would
be circumcised by a male Jewish doctor *l'shem brit* (for conversion
purposes). I wanted to set up an appointment for *beit din* (rabbinical
court to approve the conversion) and . . . *mikveh* (ritual immersion).

"*Howwww daaaaare you*," he boomed over the phone.

"Excuse me?"

"Rabbi Y might know you, but the other members of the court
do not. We may or may not approve this conversion. If you do not
get our approval, there is no need for *mikveh* now, is there? Uh, is
it *Miss* Silverman?"

"It's *Rabbi* Silverman," I said.

"Well, then. Let me explain to you how conversion works."

My heart filled with hate.

"First," he continued, "there is the *beit din*. If, and only if, the
beit din approves the conversion, there is immersion in the *mikveh*."

Pomposity masked as piety. My favorite.

Of course they could refuse us. While we would be sending Adar
to Jewish day school, it would not be Orthodox. We were observant
of Jewish ways, yet we ate cheese without Orthodox kosher certification. We celebrated the Sabbath, yet we drove the car to synagogue.

I thought about calling the Unitarians.

Over Shabbat dinner that week, I told our friends Barbara and
Brian about the phone call. They reacted as if I had announced I
was posing for the "Women of the Rabbinate" issue of *Playboy*.
(Favorite Book: The Torah. My Perfect Date: Baking challah on a
rainy afternoon.)

"Why *would* you remove yourselves from your community by seeking an Orthodox *heksher* (religious certification)?" asked Barbara, a Reconstructionist rabbi.

The bigger kids finished eating and went to play in the living room. Adar toddled around the table visiting a smile upon each of us.

"I'm with you, by the way," Yosef said to Barbara and Brian. "Those people's Jewishness is no more authentic or authoritative than ours. Remember God's 'voices'—*plural*—at Sinai? *One voice came out of Me which split into countless voices*, one for each person's contexts and strengths."

"An eighth grade Jewish education is a dangerous thing," I said.

"*When I spoke to the prophets I multiplied visions*," said Barbara, quoting from the book of Hosea. "To which the rabbis said, 'For among all of them the experience in prophesy of one is not like the experience in prophesy of another.'"

"At least *she's* a rabbi!" I said to Yosef.

"Frankly, I cannot think of any reason I'd agree with you, Susan," said Barbara. "But go ahead, tell us your thoughts."

"I understand what you're saying, all of you," I said. "But this isn't about God, or about us. It's about protecting Adari." I pulled him onto my lap. "He'll never know who his birth parents were, or their religion and ethnicity. He will never know if he has birth siblings. He will never know the circumstances of his birth and the early weeks of life. There are so many holes we can't fill. I don't want anyone to be able to cast doubt on his Jewish identity."

"You'd sacrifice yourself and your ideals to the Orthodox claim of sole authenticity?" asked Brian.

"I'm willing to pay with our own souls, in a sense, in return for an insurance policy against the schmucks who would question Adar's Jewish identity. I'll pay off the neighborhood bullies for their promise not to harass him for his kosher-lunch money. Can you imagine him getting to the Jewish high school and at the Orthodox morning services they don't let him have an *aliyah* (blessing for reading the Torah)? Or some girl's—or boy's!—parents refuse to let him date their child because they don't accept the authenticity of his conversion?"

"I have to admit, I get it," Barbara said.

"I don't know," said Brian, a social justice lawyer. "I understand your feelings about it, but I'm still uncomfortable that you're caving to their bullying."

"And to an understanding of God's will that's limited to their interpretation," Barbara added. "Come on, this is *your* mantra—a limited vision of God is a form of idolatry. They're worshiping the image they've created in their minds."

I did feel, in a way, as if I were betraying God by going to a rabbinic court that thought it knew what God wanted. If you can know God, then God had to be small enough to know. That's idolatry.

Even Aliza felt empowered to challenge Jewish traditions and God. But when it came to Adar, I lost faith in our complex, multi-layered Jewish process and clung to the Golden Calf of Orthodoxy. I had smashed the tablets of our Torah, and it took a long time to risk bringing down a new set. We would not complete Adar's conversion process for six years.

Circumcision, on the other hand, could not wait. Early the next Friday, I bundled Adar in the blue L.L. Bean snowsuit with the pink and purple flowers, handed down from each of his sisters in turn. "It's not enough that he's black and Jewish, he also has to be dressed like a girl?" said my friend Lisa. But the snowsuit was warm and waterproof, and Adar looked so beautiful in it. I fastened the Velcro below his chin, adjusted the hood above his eyebrows, and dabbed Vaseline on his cheeks, lips, and nose to protect his skin from getting chapped. Arms wide at his sides, Adar was too puffy to fit in his car seat.

Yosef drove so he could go straight to work after, but Adar and I would walk the few blocks to the hospital for his circumcision. Never was this irrational, irreversible, and dramatic act in question. We would cast Adar's lot with the Jewish people via his penis—causing him discomfort and permanently altering his body. Talk about chutzpah.

I was a child when I first understood circumcision, and as a Jewish practice in particular. My mother told me that in Europe, where her mother came from, Jewish boys were fearful and secretive in the gym showers because their circumcisions would "give them away" as Jews. I felt a kinship with those boys. It fit perfectly with the worldview I was forming. Circumcision was our sign of, well, *brotherhood* with the oppressed, a symbol of a Jew's obligation to repair the world. Just as human beings have the power to imperfectly perfect the physical aspects of their bodies through circumcision, so too we can perfect the world through righteous action.

The penis is a symbol of future generations, as well as an actor in making them. Circumcising a Jewish penis is making a covenant with God that future generations will be Jewish. Claiming Adar for the Jewish people was one thing. We also claimed his children, our grandchildren and great-grandchildren, who would also be the biological descendants of a family lineage we would never know. And it's not bad to remind men that, as a sex, their penises are subject to cultural norms, not drivers of them.

I walked briskly, pushing Adar in his stroller. To our right, snow banks, gray with salt and soot, encroached on the sidewalk. To our left, trees were bare and rigid. A garbage truck passed, and Adar twisted his bulkiness around to look. I stopped so he could feast his eyes on it. The truck disappeared, he turned forward, and we continued on.

Our merged shadows preceded us on the frozen glare of the sidewalk. For me it was a murky shadow of doubt cast by this ancient rite. Imagine the shock of our biblical ancestors Abraham and Sarah when God's promise of a son was followed by this little surprise: "You shall circumcise the flesh of your foreskin, and that shall be the sign of the covenant between you and Me. And throughout the generations, every male among you shall be circumcised at the age of eight days."

I could see Abraham in the doorway of his tent, chatting with God. "Cut off my what?"

As Yosef and I were shown to a small room in the busy, overheated surgical ward, my heart rate increased. We were, at least momentarily, harming this little boy who was happily allowing me to undress him on the gurney. Before removing his diaper, I kissed his tummy. He laughed and put his hands on my cheeks. Even as an infant, Adar's muscles were strong and defined, like a little man.

"Bye bye, baby foreskin," I said, waving at my son's crotch. Someone had told me that it might be used in cosmetic surgery. "Maybe you'll find a nice home on a rich woman's nose."

"I think it's for skin grafts, honey," Yosef said.

"Then maybe you'll be on the lips of a great rabbi, in a black suit, with side curls and a fedora, who burned his lips sneaking a cigarette on Shabbat," I said. "You'll help teach about the holy covenant of penile alteration and how someone wrote in a book that God commanded it so we did it to millions of baby boys over thousands of years."

The surgeon arrived. We made sure ahead of time he was Jewish, so that as far as this particular procedure was concerned, he was kosher. He was also male, as per my request, in case we did go with an Orthodox conversion.

Yosef and I accompanied the stretcher into the operating room, holding Adar's little hands as we walked. The anesthesiologist put a mask over Adar's mouth and nose. Yosef put on a white yarmulke, embroidered in red, purple and gold thread by Ethiopian Jews. I kissed Adar's forehead as his lids slid closed over his wide black eyes. Yosef and I recited the blessing that accompanies ritual circumcision.

Blessed are You, Adonai our God, Ruler of the universe, who has sanctified us with Your commandments, and has commanded us to enter our children into the covenant of Abraham, and, we added, *Sarah.*

Back in our little curtained-off area in the ward, I sat in the easy chair. "I'm a little freaked out right now," I said. "He won't die in there, right?"

"I'm actually really happy," Yosef said. "I feel like this is a new connection for me and Adar. He'll be circumcised because I am. It's another step in claiming him as my son."

Later, I sat in a chair with Adar's head on my shoulder. He opened his eyes but cried inconsolably as if from a nightmare. He pulled away from my embrace, something he hadn't done since Fitsum first handed him to me.

"Mama's here," I said. "Mama's here, my baby."

"It's not pain," the nurse explained. "He's disoriented from the anesthesia."

I was furious at this stupid tradition. Like Abraham, we led a trusting son to a modern-day altar to enact a covenant that he could not yet understand, the sacrifice of a small part of his body. Perhaps it's a reminder of the irrational and destructive force that can come of faith if we are not vigilant. Or, to men, that the penis is not God. But, like Isaac's mother, Sarah, I was not happy about it. When she heard of her son's binding on an altar, that her own husband had lifted the knife above him, the rabbis say: "She uttered six cries, corresponding to the six blasts of the shofar." The shofar here is ironic: Sarah's actually screaming at God: "Now *you* listen to *me*, buddy!"

Yosef went off to his job. As I wheeled Adar home, he fell into a deep sleep in his stroller, undisturbed by bumps and jolts over the ice and snow. We had put him under anesthesia and drawn his blood to meet an ancient ritual. *It's barbaric. We should be arrested. Judaism sucks.*

As I passed the synagogue next to our house, the rabbi was driving in. "Adar was just circumcised," I announced.

"*Mazel tov*," he said joyfully.

That evening, candles flickered on the windowsill and the aroma of hot food filled the room. I began to feel better as Yosef, the girls, and our friends gathered at the table. Adar sat on my lap, relaxed.

"Are you okay, baby?" Aliza asked, holding his hands.

"What a day you had," friends cooed in his direction.

Hallel sidled up to me, taking one of my arms off Adar and wrapping it around her. "Mama," she said.

"Yes, sweetie?"

"I have a headache in my penis, too."

I didn't want to laugh at her, so I made compassionate noises and invited her to help me sing the blessing over the wine. "Why don't you take the challah cover off and say *hamotzie* (the blessing over bread)?" I said to Hallel.

She lifted the cover and I noticed that the heel of the bread had been cut off. Bewildered, I looked up at Yosef, who grinned back in delight. I scanned the food on the table: challah, asparagus, green beans, even the lasagna. He had cut the tips off of everything.

Chapter 15

The Missing Piece

For Adar, hiding wasn't a way to vanish. It was a way to appear.

"Wayaz Adawi?" a tiny disembodied voice calls from behind the couch, signaling me to find him.

I put my hands on my hips, scan the room, and wonder aloud, "Where IS Adari? In a drawer? No . . . On the bookshelf? No . . . "

My heart is stretched to bursting in its pull toward him: his soft cheek against mine, his arms surprisingly strong, his hands imprinting themselves on my shoulder blades, the kiss I will plant with a long *mm-mwah* on his silky forehead. This is his story of becoming my son. He jumps out from behind the couch—a toddler Sammy Davis Jr. after a big number—huge smile, arms outstretched. *I gotta be meeeeee!*

Cue the lights, the applause, the laughter, and that big hug. Here you are, our hug says to each other. Always here. Always mine. *Every exile has a homecoming.*

Or not.

"Mama, wayaz my tummy-mommy?" he asks, his nose against mine.

"I don't know, sweetie," I say, bracing myself, gathering my thoughts. "Sometimes I wonder about her too."

Every night when he was four, his last year in nursery school, Adar pulled the same book from his shelf, handed it to me, climbed onto his bed, and nestled under my arm, leaning into me.

"It was missing a piece," I read to Adar from his storybook.

Even though he could not yet read, Adar turned each page at the right time. The sparse illustrations prompted him to recite the prose along with me, word for word. "And it was not happy. So it set off in search of its missing piece," he said solemnly.

Shel Silverstein's story in *The Missing Piece* is about a circle, drawn with sparse black lines on a white page, with a missing piece the shape and relative size of a pizza slice. The circle goes on a journey in search of its missing piece, traveling through rain and snow and hot sun, finding pieces that either don't fit or *don't want to be anyone's missing piece.*

"How come it doesn't want to be someone's piece?" Adari asked.

"I don't know," I answered. Neither of us could understand not wanting to belong to someone.

Because it was incomplete, the circle moved slowly. As it plodded along, it smelled flowers, had a butterfly land on it, and noticed the world around, all while singing its song through a mouth formed by the errant pizza slice: *Oh I'm looking for my missing piece, hi-dee-ho, here I go, looking for my missing piece.*

Adari took cover under my shirt. "Pretend I'm in your tummy," he said. He was small enough to fit his whole little body under my loose top. He folded his arms and bent his knees to his chest, his eyes peering out at my throat as he carefully covered each toe with my shirt hem.

This was not our first time pretending I was pregnant with Adar. Often at bedtime he'd look out through the stretched neckline of my T-shirt and whisper his initial command, "Pretend you're walking." Lying supine on Adari's bed under his warm, soft weight, I would move my feet as if strolling along the sidewalk. Peeking through my neckline he would again direct me, "Now you see someone you know."

"Hi, how are you?" I said obligingly. "Oh, me? I'm fine. Just taking a walk with my baby in my tummy! Okay, bye."

"Now you're walking again," he would say. "Now you see someone you know."

"Hi, Auntie Laura. Yup, I'm just taking a walk with my baby in my tummy!"

"Can I really go inside your tummy?" Adari asked, his big eyes wide at my chin.

"You can pretend, but you can't *really* go inside my tummy," I explained.

"Why? What's *in* there?" he demanded as if some sixth sense had set off internal alarms, flashing and wailing like the spacecraft in *Aliens*. His eyebrows scrunched in his telltale mix of concern and curiosity. Funny, because Yosef and I had just been talking about having another birth child soon.

We lay smushed together on his single bed, his pile of storybooks stacked beside us on the green nightstand. In the soft light that glowed through a pale yellow lampshade, we looked at each other. I felt found out. I gently pulled his head onto my shoulder and kissed it.

"Mommy?"

"Mmm."

"Who's my tummy-mommy?"

"I don't know," I said quietly. My eyes welled with tears. Many times I had begged God to let her know that her son, our son, was safe and loved. While my sorrow was genuine, it was also vain and indulgent, an illusion of redemption from my complicity in the world's pain that played itself out all too sharply in another woman's life—if she was still alive.

"Why? Nobody knows her?"

"Well, nobody we know knows her."

"Did my tummy-mommy keep me?" Adar continued.

"No," I said gently as I slipped my arm under his upper back, wondering what he meant. I should have asked.

He adjusted his head onto my shoulder. "Did she nurse me?"

"I don't know, sweetie."

"Did it hurt my tummy-mommy when I was born?"

"Childbirth hurts for a while," I said vaguely, vamping.

"Is she dead?"

She could be wondering the same of Adar right now. She must have feared his death.

Looking into my eyes, his face serious and thoughtful, Adar asked if his tummy-mommy was my friend Sally, whose brown skin might have prompted this theory.

"I grew in Sally's tummy and then she brought me to Ethiopia and then Mommy and Abba came to get me," he announced.

"No, sweetie," I said, managing not to laugh. "Sally is not your tummy-mommy."

"Maybe a lion ate me up and then pooped me out in Ethiopia." Now I laughed. Poop is funny.

He looked at me gravely, and I bit the inside of my cheeks.

"One person we know met her," he said.

"Really, honey?" I lifted my head to see his whole face. "Who was that?"

"Me. When I was born."

"Oh, my God. You're right, sweetie. *You* met her." I pulled his blanket around him more snugly.

"But I don't remember her," he said quietly, lowering his gaze.

"Oh, my sweet boy," I said, turning his face toward me and holding each cheek in my open hands. "No one ever remembers when they were babies."

There was no remembering for him, no recollection of a face or the anchor of a story. No who or what or how or why to understand his coming to be. And I had none of that to give him. I had only a messy mosaic of stories—our family inside the unwieldy unfolding narrative of the Jewish people—within which he could weave his life. Appreciating mystery is the only way I could honestly approach Adar's origins. It was the only way I could fathom God. In this way, Adar was a portal to *kedusha*—holiness. *I Will Be What I Will Be* was God's answer to Moses's question, "Who Are You?" God-as-future. God-as-becoming. Moses's future was becoming known, even as his origins were unknown to him. How could he have remembered his mother, Yocheved, placing him in a basket she had lined with bitumen and pitch, the small boat in which the river would carry him away from the Egyptian edict of death. How did she get her hands to obey her intention and let go of that basket? My deepest fears formed themselves into prayer even when I was simply buckling my child into his car seat.

Moses's cry carried beyond the hum and thrum of the river, and pierced the conversation of Pharaoh's daughter and her handmaids as they bathed. Thus, the grown daughter of Pharaoh "heard the cries of the child." Tragically, inexplicably, Yocheved hid herself in order to save her child. Perhaps Adar's birth mother prepared him in a basket, wrapped and warm, protected from mosquitoes, sun, and rain. Perhaps she, like the woman who released Moses to the Nile's flow, "stationed herself at a distance" to ensure his safety as long as she could. But never did Adar's birth mother get to "lift her eyes" to redemption, at least not with him.

She and I were a team, like Yocheved and Pharaoh's daughter. Did Yocheved call out for her son Moses once he was ensconced in Pharaoh's palace? Did the daughter of Pharaoh, raising her beautiful, wise boy, cry for Yocheved's loss?

Oh, Adari. Your birth mother has taken her place in the long line of women who could only save their children by leaving them. Our tapestry of stories has raw, ragged holes.

And now a bedtime story. I held him tightly, his head on my chest as we read aloud together. Toward the end, the circle finds its missing piece. Now a complete circle, it gains momentum and rolls along *so fast it could not stop to talk to a worm or smell a flower, too fast for a butterfly to land.*

Aha, the circle says, *so that's how it is,* and gently sets the piece down.

Chapter 16

Big Bang Gal

*H*ere is the big question: Why did God create an ideal, orderly universe and then make it impossible for me to clean my kitchen?

I managed to compile a neat-ish stack of strewn mail, random papers, and school forms, while ignoring the mouse droppings behind the garbage can. Now I had to find enough clear counter space to open a can of tomato sauce for the spaghetti that I would put on the stove once I cleaned the pot from last night's dinner.

"Aliza Rose! Honey, get your homework ready. I'll sit with you in a few minutes." Aliza was in second grade and had already established avoidance habits. Avoidance was hard work; I remember slogging through years of it myself.

She sat at the table with her backpack on the floor and pulled duct tape off her big toe. "Ouch!" she said, sucking in her breath through her teeth. The wart she had been battling for days had come off. She held it up between thumb and forefinger. "I'm gonna put its head on a toothpick as a warning to the others," she said.

After you do your homework.

Hallel wanted my help with her kindergarten artwork. "Mama, is there some string? Where's the tape?" I weighed the odds of her finding the big scissors before I filled a pot with water and got it on the stove.

I surveyed the landscape: spaghetti on the ready, dishes in the sink smeared with a spilled thermos of vegetable soup, a half-eaten banana in its blackened peel, soggy crackers, and three backpacks lying dead on the kitchen floor. Each backpack was a portable eco-system—a collection of papers, natural treasures (heavy rocks were a favorite), art-in-progress, and greasy, smelly lunchboxes. Unleashing the remains of their school lunches into the garbage disposal could send a feral cat retching. I could hear my mother's voice, "You need to teach those kids to put their own things away." Order was easy in theory, hard in practice.

Unless you're God, Who immediately categorized everything. Sea and sky, light and darkness, day and night. I'm more of a Big Bang gal—everything scattering outward at the speed of light.

"Order" is another abstract noun, like love, peace, happiness, and loyalty. It doesn't exist in an absolute form outside of God, but I am as addicted to its promise as I am resentful of its pull on me.

"I'm hungry," Hallel complained. "Can I have some veggie links?"

"Baby, I'm not cooking anything else right now. Why don't you go sit with Adari in the family room? I have to do homework with Aliza until Abba comes home. Then we'll eat."

We set up Aliza's homework station in the living room, as per the advice of her teacher. A cleared table upon which we carefully arranged tea in the frog-shaped ceramic pot we chose for this purpose, plus pencils, pens, highlighters, paper clips, all the Staples paraphernalia that gives a false sense of competence.

Aliza's hair was in her face. Her glasses hung to the end of her nose. Her pages were crumpled, half her folders were missing, and she kept placing her teacup on top of her math book, leaving damp light-brown rings. How did this insightful, empathic, articulate, and creative child become such an academic mess?

"Okay, sweetie, let's sharpen this pencil and try the first word problem," I said.

As Aliza failed to connect in any meaningful way with her assignments, I felt forsaken from my rightful place as mother to a high-achieving child. I didn't even realize my own assumptions, that my kids would naturally be the most advanced in their class, until she was sent for tests to determine if she had learning disabilities.

The test was given through the local public school. Aliza and I met with the very personable and professional school psychologist who administered the reading test. She gave Aliza a tall, thin picture book with one or two sentences at the bottom of every page. *Mommy and Me* told the story of a little girl doing activities with her mother. *I like to shop with my mommy. I like to ride bikes with my mommy. I like to sing songs with my mommy.* It took what felt like an hour for Aliza to read this book out loud, and even then with lots of mistakes. I felt sick. What does this mean? Can she stay at the Jewish school? Will she pass the standardized tests? Who will marry her?

"Okay, Aliza," said the tester. "What does a little girl like to do with her mommy?"

Aliza, unperturbed by her poor performance, looked the woman in the eye and happily said, "Save the people in Bosnia?"

The genocide in Bosnia was a topic of conversation in our house, and Aliza had dictated to me a letter to President Clinton. The psychologist smiled, turned her head to me, and barely not laughing, said, "I don't know how to score that."

That was the problem. This child didn't play by the rules that were handed down at Suburban Sinai: Do well in school, go to an excellent college, and then you can have a good life. How was I going to get her to meet these standards? If she didn't, she'd fall off the edge of the world, and I wouldn't be able to save her.

I was falling off the world anyway. Once Yosef was home, I handed homework management over to him and returned to the kitchen to once again improvise the dinner dance for which I still had no established choreography. Pirouette to the fridge, plié to retrieve a probably still okay piece of cheese, arabesque to reach for the cold cooked spaghetti as I close the fridge with my foot. A less than graceful show.

Adari came into the kitchen. He stood with his legs apart and his arms spread at his sides. *I gotta be meee!* His tiny white sneakers with red fire trucks on the sides made my heart swell.

"Mama!" he proclaimed.

"Hi, sweetie."

"Come! Come!"

Where I saw a kitchen in need of attention, he saw a black hole that sucked his mother into infinity. He tried to rescue me by pulling my hand toward the family room to play. In theory I wanted that, too. I wanted the building blocks of our days and years to be constructed of playing together, conversations, quiet games, singing, and parading around to our CD of lively children's folk songs.

When Aliza was an infant, I said to Yosef, "I want to raise her so that even if she spends her elder years alone, God forbid, in a nursing home, she will have a light in her soul that keeps her feeling cherished and strong." I think that to do that, I would have to stop and look at them sometimes. Play a game. Laugh a little. Nourish their budding souls through the light of my eyes, a human photosynthesis. Not just give them the sight of my back and the finger (index, that is, indicating *hold on a minute*).

Adar added a new dimension to the old tension between housework and spending time with the kids. He put our lives into a larger perspective, one that included faraway people and continents—a world of poverty, an unreachable birth mother. And here I stood with this child before me, healthy and happy and loved, beckoning me as he stood in the kitchen wearing remnants of his day-care activities on his clothes. Wasn't there some cosmic necessity that I swoop him up, kiss his cheeks, and go play?

I could see which color paints he used in preschool and the peanut butter he had for lunch. His pants pockets and seams bore evidence of how much time he had spent digging in the sandbox. I made a mental note for bath time: remove shoes and socks carefully so the sand doesn't spill everywhere. His feet were beautiful, still so soft on the soles. I would take a few moments as I got him changed into pajamas to kiss his fingers and toes, to breathe in his sweetness.

Adar held within him a world of disparity and contradiction—gratitude and blame and hope and fear—that could be cracked open like an egg, exposing its spiritual and physical contours. He stood there challenging me to create sacred moments in an imperfect, broken world. Our small daily needs swirled with big truths in an existential eddy. Biblical creation starts with *b'reishit*, "in the beginning." If you separate the first letter, *bet*, from the rest of the word, it becomes "there are two beginnings." A Hasidic master reads it that way. The first beginning is the divine potential that God made in the original week of creation. The second is our ongoing formation of that potential. God created sound; we form it into the blasts of the shofar, speech and prayer. I have my own chaos to shape into love and family.

Turning down the gas flame, I went with Adar to the family room. Just for a minute. We danced a song and built a block tower, creating a brief habitat, just the two of us. Back on the home planet, pasta softened in hot water, remnants hardened on dirty plates, and backpacks evolved into new life-forms.

Hallel filled the tub with copious amounts of bubble soap. "You want crazy hair, big boy?" she asked Adar as she joined him in the tub. They plopped bubble hats and painted bubble beards on each other, laughing uproariously. Hallel's pale skin shone pink from the warmth, while Adar's red tones shimmered along his smooth brown shoulders. The long bath soaked off four days of dirt from our semi-annual trip to a farm in upstate New York. We went there for the spring holiday of Shavuot, commemorating the giving of the Torah at Mount Sinai, and now, in the fall, for Sukkot, the holiday of *sukkahs* (temporary shelters). We joined twenty friends and their kids, all born into this tradition except for Adar, who entered into it as a one-year-old. We prayed outdoors in a field of grass and flowers, our prayer shawls blowing in the light breeze and our voices rising and falling with the inflection of the liturgy. Adar left the canopy of Yosef's *tallit* and bounded over to an unfurled purple yoga mat. He fell to his knees and rolled the ends of the mat inward, scroll-like, and then lifted it into his arms, the top resting on his shoulder. He stood with it and marched in a wide circle, singing *Torah, Torah, Torah* . . . the liturgical tune perfectly rendered. The group offered a chorus of loving laughter and whispered exclamations: *Look, he's making a Torah! Oh, Susie. Yosef, look!*

Faith is practice infused with grace.

At four, Adar was still little enough to swoop out of the tub into a fluffy towel and be carried like a baby. I dumped him on my big bed, the meeting place for bathed children. Before the trip to the farm I had changed the duvet cover from the floral one I used from Passover until Sukkot to the light brown of fall and winter. It smelled of the packet of my mother's vanilla beads.

Adari sat on our bed wearing only his nighttime pull-up. His long corkscrew curls were damp and sparkly from detangling spray. I squeezed Neutrogena on my hands, rubbed them together to warm the lotion, and spread it on his back, tummy, arms, legs and face to prevent the flaky dryness he got in winter.

"Mommy," he said, looking at his lotion-smeared leg. "I'm brown."

"Yes, you are," I agreed.

"Mommy?"

"Yes?"

"I don't *wanna* be brown."

"Well?" I said tentatively, inwardly chastising myself for not reading all the literature about raising children who are transracially adopted. I pictured the books lined up on the shelf, categorized but unread. They stared at me, calling me a bad mother, rolling their eyes whenever I walked by. I would later give them away. Take *that*, you bitchy judgmental books.

"Honey, what color do you want to be?" I asked.

"I wanna be purple," he said. "Like Barney."

Spared for now. Still, I rubbed the white cream until it completely disappeared. I didn't want him to think I was trying to lighten his skin.

Aliza, nine, and Hallel, seven, were brushing their teeth, naked, in the adjacent bathroom. Aliza was singing loudly: *It's getting hot in here, so take off all your clothes. I am gettin' so hot, I wanna take my clothes off.* Yosef popped his head into the bedroom. "Can we remind the babysitter to stop listening to the hip-hop station with the kids in the car?" he said. I blew him a kiss.

Hallel, still undressed, came and stood in the doorway, her eyes narrowed and her hands on her hips. With the hall light behind her she looked like a poster for *The Omen*.

"Mommy, Aliza is singing but she won't let me sing too," she said.

I grinned. Irritable nudity is funny.

The daytime thaw had given way to an evening frost, and the radiators clanked against the chill. As I zipped up Adar's leopard-print pajama blanket—the same one Aliza and Hallel had worn—he said, "Mommy, what color is Aliza?"

"Tan," I said without hesitation.

"What color is Hallel?"

"Pink."

"What color are you?"

"Off-white."

"What color is Abba?"

"Ummm. Olive."

How brilliant! Giving each of us our own color would dilute Adar's sense of difference.

The girls debated their assigned shades. "I'm not *pink*," said Hallel, her face scrunched up in a giggle.

"Isn't tan the same as off-white?" asked Aliza, examining her forearm.

I listened, pleased with my Solomon-like wisdom.

"*What* color is everyone?" Adar asked, urging me to run down the roster again.

Wait, which girl did I say was tan? Yosef was olive, right? I didn't have to search my memory for "brown," though. Hallel and Aliza took their places on my bed. I brushed Hallel's long golden waves, added the leave-in conditioner with the rosemary scent to ward off lice—less obtrusive than a head of garlic on a cross—and braided two plaits. Next was Aliza. *Braids or ponytails? Barrettes or elastics? What color? What style? How about a red ribbon to go with tomorrow's yellow shirt?*

Now that their hair was clean, untangled, and neatly swept from their faces, I felt like a capable mother again. My world was in order, like God's first creation. *And God saw all that He had made and found it very good.*

Hold this moment.

"Mommy?" Adar asked. "Will you brush my hair like you brush theirs?"

For Adar, hair care was tedious and practical—each wet curl unraveled and untangled before freeing it to spin into itself again. Adar was the only child who didn't have long hair like mine, the only one who didn't get his hair primped by Mommy on her big bed.

It was the kind of gray September afternoon where clouds block the exacting rays of expectation, as if we exist in the biblical *tohu vavohu*—the unformed space that preceded the six days of creation. I was an hour from home, wandering rows of fruit with my family, feeling released from the details of my life. Rainy days made no demands. But my son did.

"I'm. Not. Moving." Adar sat below an apple tree. The little green apples seemed too tight for the life force within them, as if they might suddenly explode. Yet there was also something vulnerable about them hanging by their slight stems from the branches above my four-year-old.

"I don't want to ask again, sweetie," I said, standing beside the wooden wagon we had filled with red, yellow, and green apples, baskets of fresh orchard apples to dip in honey for Rosh Hashana. I loved the image of them in bowls atop our fall foliage cloth on the dining room table. "Come on, let's go."

Squatting against the slim trunk, jaw set hard, eyes on the ground, Adar crossed his arms. It was as if he had taken some sort of deranged yoga class and was practicing the "go to hell" pose. I was on the verge of the loftiest of parenting models: the plea and threat combination. I might even have been preparing for a triple: plea, threat, and bribe, although I wasn't feeling generous enough to offer a treat.

"I want to pull the wagon up the hill, but it's too bumpy!" he said.

He had been the happy horse, pulling the wagon with the slat-ted, splintery wood sides, full of sisters and apples, until he encountered some jags. Hard as he pulled, his little body just couldn't get the wheels to turn. The girls had popped out and run ahead to the car.

Adari was bereft. What kind of horse loses its riders?

"Sweetie, all options are open to you. You can pull the wagon with the apples in it, or you and I together can try to pull the wagon with the apples and the girls in it, or you can get in the wagon with the apples and I'll give you a ride."

"No!"

Hallel called to us from the parking lot: "Just! Follow! My! Voice!" she bellowed, although we could see her through the sparse saplings.

"Hallel thinks we're lost," I said. "Isn't that funny?"

Finally, I picked him up under one arm and carried him, kicking, while I pulled the wagon with my other hand. In the field between the orchard and the parking lot, I put him down on the grass to catch my breath before dragging him the rest of the way. In the open space, I looked at him for a moment, a very little boy in a very big world: *chalal*, empty space.

Two nights earlier Adar had made himself into a small, impenetrable ball. "Kids said I'm different 'cause I'm brown," he wailed. "I want to change my skin."

"Oh, sweetie, who said that?"

He turned away from me, and gave a garbled, "I don't know."

"Was it someone in your class?"

"No."

"Was it an older kid?" Ignoring my better instinct to just listen, I demanded answers. I demanded them gently, but I was out to satisfy my need for the names, ranks, and serial numbers of the elementary school enemies.

"I don't know."

"Was it a little brother or sister at pick-up time? Maybe a preschooler?"

"I don't know."

"So it was no one you knew . . . "

I was hunched over him as he lay on his side with his back to me, his arms wrapped around his shins and his head bent into his knees as I tried to package his emotions into something formed and articulate. Who said these things to you? What did they say? When did this happen?

I needed to back off and make room for Adar to struggle without my demanding clean answers. In the act of creation, say the mystics, God draws inward, making a void in which the world can become. Sometimes retreat is an act of love.

Although I have never worn makeup, and would never spend $30 on two ounces of eye cream, I sometimes play with the cleansers and moisturizers that my three sisters, all of them in the entertainment industry, leave behind after visiting. One evening, Adari was watching in fascination from the doorway as I used a citrus facial scrub and followed it with a dab of rich, silky cream from a tiny jar.

"Mama, is that only for grown-ups?" he asked.

"Oh, yeah, honey. Kids don't need it. You definitely don't need it. Your skin is perfect."

"My skin is NOT perfect!" he burst out. "I hate my skin!"

As I put the jars and creams away in the medicine cabinet, I knew that the subject was not closed.

"Mommy, how come when someone asks God for something She doesn't give it to him even if he's a good boy who asks for it," he said. When he called God a She, as I had taught him, I felt a surge of guilt. Not only was Adar different from his family, he was different from God. Was I making him as alienated from his spiritual source as he was from his biological source? My control in the creation of Adar's world was all too apparent. It usually went under the radar of our daily lives, but when you rewrite God, it's hard to miss.

I stood with Adari by my bed, wondering if it was a good idea to give him an opportunity to express his feelings again. Or would I be baiting him? One way could be healing and the other destructive—but I couldn't be sure which was which.

This happened all the time. Hallel leans back on her chair again and falls again. Do I point out the obvious? Ignore it? Comfort her? Aliza calls from school because she's tired and has a headache. If I bring her home, I wonder if she's avoiding something at school. If I make her "stick it out," I wonder if she's actually suffering, bewildered by her mother's unwillingness to take care of her.

When Aliza was small, I thought about keeping a therapy jour-
nal for her. I would write down everything that might have trau-
matized her. I could do it for each child—what a gift to them later
in life when they took their journals to their shrinks!

*Aliza, age two: forced her to finish jar of banana plum baby food, not
for her own good but mine. If she's full, she'll nap longer. (Note in case of
future eating disorder, sleep disorder, or fear of plums.)*

*Hallel, third birthday: Weaned her. Had final breast-feeding and
tried to make celebration. Consistently denied her pleas for more, except
when I gave in. (Note in case of teenage reversion to use of baby bottle,
or alcoholism, or insincere lesbianism.)*

Almost every choice a parent makes holds the possibility of positive and negative repercussions, sometimes both. We have to make
thoughtful guesses at what will be the least harmful and/or most
useful path.

Now I had an entry for Adari.

*Adar, age four: I suggested that his skin was perfect. Sent him into fit
of fury at being the only brown-skinned person in family. (Note in case
of low self-esteem, sense of alienation, or Michael Jackson obsession.)*

Adari's eyes narrowed in anger as he readied to hit or throw
something.

"Did you ask God for something, honey?" I asked him.

"Yes," he said loudly.

"What was it?"

"To make me white, but She didn't do it."

Adari's questioning was his first confrontation with God, a confrontation that would surely continue and evolve. I didn't know
where it would lead, this relationship with God that is replete with
love and resentment, joy and pain. Shouting out to God in frustration and anger is well worn in Jewish tradition, and there it was,
still innocent and unformed in the eyes of my little boy.

I had two urges: First, I did not want to argue with him. I wanted him to feel heard and to know that I could accept his feelings.

Second, I wanted to object so that he didn't interpret my silence as concurring that he would be better with white skin.

When we first decided to adopt from Ethiopia, the color difference was far from being a deterrent—it was romantic. We would appear on *Oprah*: Families Who Have Transcended Race. As Oprah prepared to introduce our family, I would adjust my halo in the dressing room mirror and rehearse a gracious smile.

But it was my bedroom mirror that reflected me now as I stood there trying to think of something not stupid to say and watching my angry, sad son climb onto my bed. His voice was loud and his enunciation purposeful, each syllable a small geyser, primal cries given phonic shape. "I hate this family," he shouted. "It's a big fat idiot family. I hate Abba, Aliza, and Hallel. I wish they were dead. Not pretend dead, really dead. I hate me."

He started throwing some of the laundry that was piled on the bed. A large red shirt unfolded into the air like a parachute and landed on the floor. He scattered a stack of children's underwear like feathers in a pillow fight. Unmatched socks flew into the window like a flock of pet parakeets trying to escape.

"I want a *brown* family," he continued. "I don't want to be in *this* family. I hate this family."

"Sweetie," I said, trying to remonstrate with Adar as he threw his tantrum. "Our family wouldn't be our family without you."

"I don't care."

Now books hit the floor as he threw my small stack of novels one by one as if he were smashing glass. "*It's a big fat idiot family*. I want a *brown* brother. Two of them, then we can be triplets. Then there will be three boys and three brown so it will be *fair*."

The unfolding realization of his differences from the rest of his family—his color, and that he had a tummy-mommy who was different from his mommy—was world altering.

I picked up the clothes and began to refold them. He was like Adam in the Garden of Eden; he was suddenly ashamed and self-conscious, no longer part of an organic, perfect world.

Adar lay his head on my pillow and, mid-accusatory-whine, fell asleep. He did that, going from fully awake to fast asleep. No drifting off for this boy. I matched the socks, with Adar splayed across my bed. I pictured him waking, like Adam when he rose for the first time after God blew breath into him, still innocent of life outside the spontaneous, natural world of our family garden. But now my four-year-old will furrow his brow and begin to forge a path and place for himself outside of a safe but superficial simplicity.

But not alone. His parents and sisters will walk out of the garden gate with him. Arguments, laughter, frustration, and enduring love would accompany us as we built a world for ourselves—a world with less innocence, but with, perhaps, a larger measure of wisdom. One with blemishes that must not be concealed—even with the most expensive cosmetics.

Chapter 17

More Eggs in the Nest

On my thirty-ninth birthday I told Yosef that I planned to be the sexiest forty year-old ever. I joined a gym, went to a hairdresser, and replaced my baggy clothes with some shapely V-necks and tighter jeans. A friend said I looked like I was getting younger. And that's when I got pregnant, on a now-or-never impulse. I was due in June 2003, one month after I turned forty.

At our friends Sharon and Shimi's house for Sabbath dinner, we discussed the increased sense of danger we had lived with since 9/11. Is the world plummeting into total chaos?

Shimi pointed to my belly and said, "You have faith in the future."

I searched my mind for some deep thing to say about the human condition.

"I just wanted more kids," I said truthfully.

On the floor of the living room, in front of the first fire of the winter, Yosef and I told the kids there was a new baby growing in mommy's tummy. The girls danced and talked nonstop. How many days until it comes? Is it a boy or a girl? What does it look like right now? Well, it's the size of a small apple and has all its body parts and even some hair. And its head is half the size of its body! Aliza showed how much of her body would be head if her head was half the size of her body, and Hallel found that highly disgusting. Adar stared at my belly as if it might reveal something. I pulled him onto my lap. The kids were nine, seven, and four and a half.

A couple of months into the pregnancy, Yosef and I took our first romantic vacation together since starting a family, the honeymoon we never had. Mali, our au pair, stayed at home with the kids. I bought a skirted maternity bathing suit, and we left icy Boston for three days at an all-inclusive resort in Jamaica. The French doors of our hotel room gave way to a balcony overlooking the beach. The evening horizon was a meld of blues and reds against the far black line of sea. There was the smell of salt and clean air, and a bonfire somewhere down the beach. Here I could forget all my anxieties.

When the phone rang my heart stopped. Oh my God, the kids were dead. It was the Newton police and they got our information from Mali's phone, I said. It's Jeffrey's death all over again, except now we're the parents who went on vacation.

Maybe it's room service, Yosef suggested helpfully.

It was my ob-gyn. "It's Dr. Roberts, I got your number from your babysitter. Sorry to call you on vacation, but I've got some disturbing news," he said. "The amnio results showed some severe abnormalities in two of the seven dishes."

"What abnormalities? What dishes?"

"It suggests a rare and severe form of mental retardation. Don't ask me to explain more, this is outside my expertise. I advise you to consult a geneticist on Monday when you get back."

The sky outside was starting to take on a neon, surreal tinge. When parents take a trip, babies die.

We called our friend Ben, a brilliant doctor and ultra mensch. "It could be a lab artifact, a problem with the culture in the petri dish," said Ben. "Given that it was only in two of the dishes, that's the most likely possibility, Susie. Really, enjoy Jamaica."

Yosef and I lay on the bed. He put his hand on my belly and looked at me. "The baby's fine," he said.

"Are you sure? How do you know?"

"The energy around the baby is good."

"What if something really is wrong?" I persisted. "If the results of a second amnio are the same, maybe we should consider abortion."

The Talmudic rabbis wrote that God made the world with ten things: wisdom, understanding, knowledge, strength, anger, might, justice, law, kindness, and mercy—attributes of God as well as the tools and materials of creation. Even with all that good planning, the rabbis teach, creation kept expanding, unbridled, beyond God's will, until He got angry and made it stop. *Ani El Shaddai*, "I am God Almighty." But the rabbis parsed the syllables differently, which radically changed the meaning: "I am God, Who said 'enough' to My world."

I didn't have all those powerful attributes in creating this fetus. I just wanted another kid. And now the creation Yosef and I had set in motion might be growing unbridled, out of my control, beyond my will, or willingness. Maybe I, too, would say "enough."

I kept abortion at the back of my mind as a way out, a bizarre comfort.

The results of the second amnio, via the geneticist—who was a lovely man, completely unlike the ob-gyn—were good. In the process, we found out we were having a girl, which was also good—especially, I felt, for Adar. Girls come from Mommy's body, and boys come from Ethiopia.

The crisis was averted. All was well. "Let's adopt another boy," I said to Yosef.

"Why don't we talk about that after we adjust to having four kids?" he said.

One thing I'll say, it's easier to tempt your husband into working toward a biological child than an adoptive one. "You know that this pregnancy is not instead of another adoption, right?" I reminded Yosef. "You have a big fancy professional life. Adoption is my life's mission."

I had wanted five children since I could remember, and this impulse was confirmed the moment I saw our *ketuba*, the Jewish marriage contract. We provided the artist with the text, which we wrote together, and some guidelines: We wanted the walls of the Old City of Jerusalem, and above each of the seven gates we assigned a traditional quote. Outside the walls the artist drew representations of holidays. For Shavuot, she drew five children dancing with the Torah.

"Look, we're going to have five children," I told Yosef as we marveled at the beautiful illustration.

I began telling friends and family that we would adopt another boy. "Why do you want a three- or four-year-old and not a baby?" they asked.

"That's where we have an opening," I told them. The four-year gap between Adar and the new baby was calling out to be bridged. Adar was calling out for a brother, someone who looked like him.

Aliza's bedside light illuminated the floor-to-ceiling mural of a tree my mother had originally painted for Adar. *Eitz chayim hee,* "it's a tree of life," as the book of Proverbs says of Torah. Torah is a tree whose roots are in heaven but whose branches bear fruit on earth. Humanity's initial rupture was because of a tree—the tree of knowledge of good and of evil.

In the nook between the trunk and the largest branch, my mother had painted a nest with three eggs, and a bluebird watching over them. I looked to the three fragile, life-filled eggs, each a swirly light blue, each hiding and protecting a lone potential being. My mother would need to paint two more eggs in the nest.

Seven months pregnant, on a warm Sunday, I was in the kitchen when Mali came home, a stunned Aliza loping in behind her. "Mommy, a boy is dead on the street!" said Aliza.

"What?"

"We passed an accident and the boy was on the ground with his bike next to him and a woman was standing over him with her hands over her face like this," said Aliza, rushing the words, then covering her mouth with both hands and shaking her head slowly back and forth. "She had hit him and he was dead. I feel worse for her than for him."

Right then, as we were standing in our kitchen, that boy's parents and siblings were beginning the "after" period—in that horrible moment that would forever divide and define the rest of their lives. As I feared it would affect, though in a much milder way, my sweet girl. I worried about her. Her characteristic wide smile had become less frequent. She retreated into her room more. She was showing hints of a dark side. Friends had recommended a psychiatrist.

That night, Aliza called me into her room, but she was not on her bed. "Aliza? Where are you?"

"All I can see is the boy," I heard from somewhere near the window. "And that woman standing over him."

Aliza sat outside on the sloped roof of the family room, a few feet below her second-story window. She was hugging her knees to her chest.

"What are you doing?" I said, trying not to panic, not to startle her. I reached my arms through the window to beckon her.

"I feel better out here," she said, not moving.

Oh, the hole that will never be filled in some poor family. And my daughter holding an existential emptiness that is simply part of being human. I wanted her to climb back into her room, into my arms, filling that scared emptiness inside me.

But she remained perched on the roof, looking into the black sky as I stood in the window, fearing the blackness would envelop her.

Chapter 18

Holy Transgressive, Batman!

"**D**oes baby girl eat?" Adari asked.

"Yes sweetie, she eats what I eat."

I was leaning over the dining room table with a salad bowl, stretching my body upward while lowering my arm like a crane so I wouldn't knock over a wine glass with my giant belly. With one leg slightly raised behind me I felt graceful, the way I might in a yoga pose if I did yoga. Full and beautiful, like Demi Moore eight months pregnant on the cover of *Vanity Fair*.

I turned on my other foot and squatted—pliéd!—to face Adar. I held his hands and looked straight into his eyes, holding his gaze while my mind raced. I had to convey that we were unwaveringly mother-and-son. We had a holy and covenantal relationship, a promise and the fulfillment of that promise. Whenever you call, I will answer *hineini*—I am here. Here, baby, beside you, for you, utterly devoted to you. This new baby is more love for you, not less! I would *die* for you.

"Mommy?" He pointed to my heart.

"Yes my love," I said, holding his cheeks and kissing his forehead. He could sense what I felt!

"You have hummus on your booby."

As I tripled my chin to look down and wipe food off my shirt, I felt more Walmart shopper than *Vanity Fair* cover.

The long oval table had been handmade for my mother's mother over fifty years earlier. Grandma Goldie made her husband, Herman, change their name from Cohen to Halpin in the 1940s, when she still woke screaming in the night from the pogroms of her childhood in Poland. No need to advertise being Jewish, she reasoned. Now this table, with its bottle of kosher wine, two challahs, a Kiddush cup, and a tub of hummus with a boob-shaped indent, yelled out, "Jews! Jews here!"

"Did I eat what my tummy-mommy ate?" Adar asked.

"Yes," I said. "You ate what your tummy-mommy ate."

"Can I eat from *your* tummy?"

"No, but I can still feed you. And it's so much better because we can look at each other while I do!"

Umbilical cord, fork, what's the difference? They're both ways for a mommy to feed her children. In fact, I only use the umbilical cord to feed the baby so I have my hands free to take care of *you*!

Yosef and I had explained to Adari that, with God's help, this baby was made from a little egg and a tiny seed of Mama and Abba's bodies. And that when Adar was born, God took a little of Mama's soul, and a little of Abba's soul, and put them in him.

I maneuvered to the floor and sat with my legs folded in front of me, what in preschool I called "Indian style" but what Adar and his sisters had been taught to call "crisscross applesauce."

"Adari, touch here," I said, placing his hand on my right side. "Can you feel the baby's tush? Hold your palm flat."

Adari stared solemnly at his hand, staking his claim as Ashira's big brother by taking responsibility for monitoring her movement. It was a look I imagined Moses might have had—solemn, focused, ready—when he answered *hineini* to God's call from the burning bush.

"Can I be inside your tummy with baby girl?" asked Adari.

I hugged him close. *Don't be jealous of this baby! My relationship with her is strictly placental.*

Yosef and the girls came downstairs, the girls' hair still wet from a bath. Aliza, Hallel, and Adar took turns lighting candles while standing on the wide, handmade wooden chair my mother gave us. We all sang the candle blessing together, and Yosef and I blessed each one of our children. This was probably the last Friday night that we would lay our hands on, and bless, only three children.

I placed my hands on Aliza's head. She covered mine with hers and we looked into each other's eyes. All three children always blessed us back, yet each time it still somehow took me by joyful surprise. The *kohen*, the high priest in the ancient Temple, approached the Holy of Holies, the inner sanctum, every year on Yom Kippur. There he begged God to bless the people, and God responded by asking the *kohen* for a blessing. A holy and transgressive act! "May it be Your will that Your compassion outweighs Your judgment," the *kohen* said, and God nodded His head. That's what their blessings brought out in me, too: greater compassion in my godlike power over them.

At ten years old, her hands on my head, there was still baby in Aliza's face, with dimples in her wide cheeks and her glasses askew, a symbol of her consistently surprising perspective.

Yivarech'echa adonai v'yishm'recha. May God bless you and keep you.

Ya'eir adonai panav eilecha v'kunecha. May God shine upon you and be gracious to you.

Yisa adonai panav eilecha v'yaseim lecha shalom. May God look upon you and give you peace.

"Every day of your long life," Aliza added, as she always did with her hands on my cheeks, shaking my head back and forth for emphasis.

I went next to Hallel, who was reaching for the grape juice. "Not yet, honey," I said, grabbing her hand. She placed her hands on my head as I placed mine on hers. She was still eyeing the grape juice as I blessed her, and together we said amen.

When I got to Adari, I sank to my knees and put my hands on his head. He put his hands on mine and we looked at each other nose to nose. When I looked into the girls' faces I saw aspects of Yosef and me, but when I looked into Adar's face I got a closer glimpse of the divine.

As I blessed him, he placed his hand back on my belly, moving it around to feel for a discernible baby part.

"Wait!" said Aliza, jumping from her chair to join him. "May God bless you and keep you. May God look upon you and be gracious to you," she said, her hands on top of Adar's.

"Me too!" said Hallel, and ran over. Yosef stood behind me, his hands on my shoulders.

Together they said, "May God look upon you and give you peace."

I was awash in love. Aliza's and Hallel's hands had lost their baby roundness, but Adar's still had dimples instead of knuckles. They were still the hands of finger painting and patty-cake. *We're God's hands*, I told my children. We use our hands to awaken God to our loved ones, to channel God's blessing, protection, grace and peace. We promise *ahyeh-asher-ehiyeh*, I will be with you.

Together, my three children promised the same to their sister-to-be.

Aliza attended the birth along with Yosef and two midwives. She moved quietly around the room, sometimes videotaping, sometimes whispering words of encouragement, sometimes both.

The Birthing Center was Laura Ashley Land, with green calico wallpaper, Pottery Barn bedspreads, and rustic furniture. The woodsy serenity mocked my real life, so I redesigned it in my mind. Instead of a clean, plush carpet, they should have piles of laundry, lost game pieces, a Lego structure (part airplane, part dungeon), and Lite-Brite pegs waiting to stab my bare feet. Instead of the stitched quilt there'd be crumbs on stained sheets. Instead of the murmuring of midwives in the hallway, there'd be a recording of children's voices, screeching: "It's mine!" "Mo-om!!!" "Play trains with me!"

"I can't do it! I can't do it!" I screamed at the midwives, who spoke in low voices around the heart monitor.

From behind the camera Aliza's sweet voice came through her sobs. "You can do it, Mom. You can do it. I love you so much."

The baby's head crowned and the midwives became stern, calling out commands. "No, I can't!" I yelled back at them.

The baby was in distress. Finally, one of the midwives pulled my legs apart, hard, and she emerged, slightly blue. They placed an oxygen mask on her. Aliza laid down her camera and bounded over to meet her new sister. Yosef stroked Aliza's head. Hallel came in shortly after and was ecstatic, clamoring to hold the baby. Adari arrived next, and cautiously stood a foot away from the bed. "Shy" was a quality I had rarely seen in him. "Oh, it's my boy," I said. "You're a big brother. She's such a lucky baby to have you for a big brother."

My love for each of them was infinite, "the whole earth and the whole sky," as we like to say in our family. I said to the new baby what I had said the day I met Aliza: "I love you so much even though I don't know what that means yet."

We named her Ashira, "I will sing." It's found in the song of gratitude the Israelites sang as they emerged from the parted seas to freedom, in celebration of the Exodus from *Mitzrayim* (Egypt), a Hebrew word for "narrow place."

Ashira la'adonai ki ga'o ga'a. I will sing to God, Who has triumphed.

Aliza and Hallel joined the chorus of adoration for Adar, as they had been prepped to do. Laura later reported that when she asked Adar on the phone about his new sister, he had said, "She's light. Yeah," and he continued in a quiet voice, as if thinking out loud, "she's definitely white."

Now he grinned and climbed into the bed next to me, bringing his face close to Ashira's. "You know," I said to Adar, "you might be a big brother, but you'll always be my baby."

Ashira was only a few hours old when we came home. I had her wrapped in a tiny white-and-blue hospital blanket as I sat with her on the deck with my feet up. The dogwood trees were in bloom, and the rose bushes climbed the waist-high wooden planks of the porch's length. The warm air intensified the sweet smell of the flowers. Our friend Shimi arrived with his five-year-old daughter, Tali, suddenly demure in the presence of a newborn.

"Have you ever seen such a new baby, Tali?" her father asked. Slight shake of the head.

"Isn't she so tiny?" Nod.

"How many hours is she now?" Shimi asked me.

"Five," I reported. I loved being able to count her age in hours. I knew by now that the move to counting in days, weeks, months, then years was relentless, ruthless. I wanted to hold this moment, relish her infancy, pretend it was eternal. I later played the same kind of game when I clipped her tiny, clear, pointy fingernails for the first time. Between this clipping and the next, I thought, she will still be brand new.

When the time came at eight days for Ashira's *brit*—the celebration of her entrance into the covenant between the Jewish people and God—we had a large crowd at our house. Ashira's face was still a pink and white mush, with a tinge of yellow from her fading jaundice. A round, bright red hemangioma fairly glowed in the middle of her right cheek, with three white lines inside the perfect scarlet circle forming a peace sign. Some guests thought we drew it on her. Oh, please. How on earth would I organize a trip to a baby-tattoo artist? I hadn't even managed to take her in for her infant hearing test.

All the attention on Ashira was exciting, but Yosef and I worried about its effect on Adar. His arrival had been one long welcoming party, but we had not yet formalized his conversion to Judaism, and therefore hadn't had a celebration like this one for him. Adari had many reasons to resent this new baby, to fear her, and try to ignore or diminish her presence. His place in the family had been usurped; he was no longer the baby. Unlike his sisters, his body had never been nourished from mine. He had no claim to residual cells in my body that a baby leaves after birth. An umbilical cord did not connect us, or need to be severed. In a way, it had to be grown. He shared no resemblance to his sisters, who all looked like their grandparents, aunts, uncles, and each other. I feared that jealousy would inhibit Adar's love for the new baby.

Others shared this concern. Many of the guests deliberately paid more attention to Adari than to Aliza, Hallel, and even Ashira. My mother brought him a T-shirt with a picture of a boy holding a sign that read, "I'm the big brother." Our friend Barbara, the rabbi who conducted the ceremony that day, had Adar hold Ashira for the ritual naming.

Afterward, I held Ashira at the dining room table while people chatted and ate. Adari stood to my right, and gently stroked his baby sister's face while everyone ate and talked. "Hi, baby," he cooed. "I'm Adari. I'm your big brother."

Barbara's husband, Brian, came and squatted beside us. "You know what, Adari?" he said in a solemn tone, although his eyes were shining. "There's a way to find out if a baby loves you. You put your finger in the palm of her hand, and if she squeezes it, that means she loves you."

Brian held Ashira's hand in his and guided Adari's right index finger across the puffy little pads at the base of her fingers. Adari seemed willing but hesitant. Maybe he didn't want to know.

I was nervous, too; sort of like eight days earlier when I thought I would be the first woman in history to be in labor for the rest of her life. Now I was sure that Ashira would be the first baby to be born without the reflex to squeeze.

I imagined interceding like the movie hero throwing himself in the way of a cocked gun: "*Noooooooooo*!!!" I would throw my body in the way of this possible wound to my son.

When Adari's small brown finger crossed Ashira's splotchy pink palm, she closed her fingers tight and squeezed.

"Wow," said Brian, smiling. "Look how tight she's holding. She *really* loves you."

Adari couldn't suppress a grin.

Adar and his sisters drew love from the Source of Love, and shaped it into brother-and-sister-hood. *T'nu oz l'elohim*, says the psalmist. Give strength to God.

Two years later, Ashira's first full sentence was spoken as she squeezed Adar tightly around his waist. "I wuv my big budda."

Chapter 19

Calling in the Big Guns

$\mathcal{T}$he small bay window ledge in the dining room was covered with candle wax. The trees darkened outside this northwest corner window, and the four festive menorahs already showed their reflection in the leaded glass windows. Later we would light all eight candles and sing the blessings.

I sank into a semi-sweet Sunday afternoon lull. Yosef was food shopping with Ashira, now six months old. The older girls were upstairs with friends. It occurred to me that they were watching unapproved movies on their computers, but it was a trade I was willing to make in return for solitude.

I was "potchkying," taking scattered laundry, shoes, toys, and school supplies to their places, and clearing the kitchen before Yosef unloaded at least ten bags of groceries.

I carried a small stack of books from the radiator cover in the foyer—a Bible, a Hasidic commentary, and a Talmudic tract fluttering with Post-its—to the family room, my favorite room in the house. Built-in bookshelves covered two of the walls and surrounded a large window on the third. On the fourth side was a sliding glass door that opened to the rear deck. The L-shaped couch stretched in front of the two walls of bookshelves. As I climbed to put the books away, I was careful not to knock down Adar's tent, a light-blue fleece blanket that stretched from the back of the couch to a shelf. It was sleeping quarters and a bridge under which to drive his fire, dump, and cement trucks. He worked thoughtfully, periodically stopping to survey his progress. He bit his lower lip like a student taking a final exam.

Adar's red sneakers stuck out, blinking, from this soft structure. What was this creation to him? A house? A fire station? A moon landing? A fort in the wilderness? His excavation in there had yielded unexpected artifacts, because he emerged from the tent clutching large laminated photos of Aliza, Hallel, Yosef, and me. "What are these?" he asked.

"Oh, wow, I almost forgot about them," I said. "Come here."

Adar and I sat together on the couch, cuddling to defy the December cold, and examined the enlarged faces. The last of the late-afternoon sun shone through the sliding glass doors, laying a golden square on the wood floor at our feet. Adar nestled into my left side, and I held the pictures with my right. At almost five, and now a big brother, he was still my baby.

He fingered the blue yarn that laced through two punch holes at the top of each picture, the two ends hanging limply at the back. "Fitsum, who took care of you, hung them inside your crib so you could see our faces," I told him.

My mother had offered to enlarge 8" x 14" pictures of each of us to send to the orphanage while Adar was still there. "They could put them inside his crib, facing in," she said.

I wasn't interested. I hadn't wanted to be seen as a demanding American, making frivolous requests for my one child when they had so many to take care of. Also, any effort unrelated to speeding up his homecoming didn't interest me. The world was divided into two categories: things that moved the adoption process forward and things that didn't. "Besides," I said to my mother, "how will we explain to them what to do with a stack of giant laminated faces?"

She sent the photos along with instructions in English and detailed diagrams for how to hang them in the crib. I threw in a T-shirt I had worn for a day so he'd have my smell in the crib with him—another one of Mom's ideas. Yosef later asked why I didn't include one of *his* T-shirts: "What am I, chopped liver?"

Holding the pictures and Adari at the same time was disorienting. My heart suddenly felt too big for my ribcage, and the world seemed to clash with itself. My mother's trademark black permanent marker and neat block print on the back of the photos reminded me that Adar was once a foreign baby and that we had been entirely unknown to him. Yet, here we were together. Hadn't we always been mother and son?

Looking out through the dining room to the front door, I recalled how I obsessively checked the mailbox for those early, tenuous links to my son—deliveries of pictures and brief developmental reports. I pressed my lips against the long, deep brown coils of hair that sprang from his head like evidence of his innate exuberance. May I never, ever miss being in your life again, I thought. With eyes closed over hot tears, I sealed the kiss and the prayer with a cartoonish smacking sound.

Adari stared at his Baba's printed letters, like an archaeologist deciphering a faded inscription. "What does it say?" he asked.

I paused. "For Daniel.'"

He had arrived at the orphanage with no information about his birth or identity. The director, Amber, had assigned him her brother's name.

In our luxurious room at the Addis Ababa Sheraton, I had worried that we should have kept the name Daniel. He already had the beginnings of an identity, certainly recognition of his name. He had been fed, comforted, played with, and kissed as "Dani" for nine months. It was our legal right to change his name, but were we ethically, spiritually, even practically entitled to impose such a thing on him? Does a child's identity come from adoptive parents, or does it precede that? How far back does it go—to the unknown womb? When I bathed him for the first time in the large marble tub of the hotel, I used his new name. He had sat, naked and smiling, as he hit the warm, soapy water with his dimpled hands.

"Adar," I said as he played.

Splash, splash.

"Dani."

He widened his eyes and looked at me expectantly.

"Adar, Dani. Dani, Adar," I repeated, playfully poking his little chest with each name.

Now, in the cooling, darkening living room, I looked at his face for signs of emotion. Surprise? Dismay? Anger? The name Daniel represented a part of his life that we could recount for him—the nine months he had lived at African Cradle Children's Center. The name was also, however, a symbol of the unknown. Did he have a name given by his birth family? What was *their* name? Did they love him? Resent him? Did they seek to save him or just want to be rid of him?

Were they still alive?

This small pile of laminated photos with "For Daniel" written boldly across their backs was like an apparition, a visible symbol of the unseen. Adari traced the block letters with his finger. I could see he was assimilating this information by the set of his jaw and his slightly furrowed brow as he flipped between the writing and the pictures, as if it were always the other side that held the secret. "Is Daniel my *real* name?" he asked.

"They called you Daniel because they *didn't know yet* that your name was Adar," I said. "But God knew."

I threw in the God thing even though, of course, I don't know what God knows. I don't know Who God is, What God is. Now suddenly I was sure about God? But Adar's use of the word "real" in relation to his life before me made me call in the Big Guns.

"That's why I'm Adar Daniel?"

"That's why you're Adar Daniel."

The biblical Jacob was given the name "Israel," which means "struggler with God." Years after he fled his twin, Esau, he would now face this estranged brother. Alone under the night sky, fearing the coming day's encounter with Esau, an *ish* (a "man") appeared to Jacob and "wrestled with him until the rise of dawn."

Who was this *ish?* An angel? (Did God have a plan for Jacob?) A ghostly vision of Esau? (Was his brother planning to attack him?) Or another aspect of Jacob himself? (What lurked in Jacob's soul that he had to face?)

Jacob overcame the *ish*, who pleaded, "Let me go, for dawn is breaking."

"I will not let you go unless you bless me," Jacob answered.

"Your name shall no longer be only Jacob," said the *ish*, "but also Israel, for you have striven with beings divine and human and have prevailed."

The name Daniel, like the *ish*, was a symbol of the many layers that make up his self—and demanded that Adar place his life in a larger context than personal biography. He was no different from anyone else—we all are made of unknown multitudes. But he did not have the gift—or curse—of a façade to pretend otherwise. And now neither were we able to pretend.

The last of the sun gave our family room the washed-out appearance of an aged photograph. With Adar's permission, I reclaimed his fleecy tent as a blanket. The fort he had built disappeared, and we wrapped ourselves in its remains, warm and snug together. After encountering this *ish* in our now shadow-filled house, I held Adari tight. "I will not let him go," I vowed silently, "until You bless him."

Chapter 20

Chaos, According to Plan

$\mathcal{T}$hrough the large window I watched the tae kwon do class, kids aged four to twelve, all levels. Aliza was eleven and close to getting her black belt. Hallel, nine, was a green belt, Adar, five, a white belt. The room, spacious and bright, nice with a light-wood floor, had a mirror covering the wall across from where I slouched on the wooden bench, squashed between other mothers in the hallway of the Jewish Community Center. To the right of the window was a sign, Energy Arts Studio, in italicized black letters. The words elicited dreamlike images: healthy meals, family yoga practice, smooth transitioning throughout our day. Mind-body unity, interpersonal calm. Generosity and forgiveness. Energy Arts.

Bob, the tae kwon do teacher, was a tall, muscular man with very short, spiky dark hair and a cross tattooed on his right index finger. He bent on one knee to tie the shoe of a boy with a black yarmulke and yellow belt that hung to his knees. All children obeyed Bob all the time.

This setup allowed my kids and me to enjoy each other free of our usually conflicting needs and agendas. I delighted in their interactions—Aliza and Hallel, who fought at home, laughed when the momentum of Aliza's side kick unintentionally spun her full circle. The girls giggled when Adari sauntered back to his place after a successful kick. Hallel, eyes wide: "Wow, Aliza," after a high jump-kick. Helping one another when their belts came untied. Adari relied in many small ways on the care of his big sisters, practicing their moves at their own levels. I gave them a thumb's up and playfully encouraged them to stop trying to get my attention through the window. Put my kids behind a glass wall under the authority of a tae kwon do black belt, and I am in control.

It's as one-way as parenting can ever be. Like God's biblical decree "let there be light"—the creation of something defined and predetermined; chaos constrained and shaped into desired figures and processes. God created most of the world this way, by decree, each creation according to its permanent, divinely ordained plan. The sun, the moon, the stars, the trees, the fish, the plants—they all move in their ways, as if on a track, with no unique influence on their own destiny.

I gazed intently at all three kids, making sure they felt my pride as they each took a turn with Bob to kick the board or learn a new pattern. Even as I watched one child, I flicked my gaze to the others, hoping to catch their eye so they would know I was actively adoring them.

I knew it was important to all three that I watch. Aliza acted as if she didn't care, while surreptitiously checking to make sure I had my eyes on her. She peeked sideways from behind the hair hanging in her eyes, or casually glanced at the mirror to see my reflection on the bench outside.

Adar was still comfortable publicly demanding my attention. He would look and point at me, then at himself, over-articulating a silent "Watch me." He stopped beside me for a moment when he came out to the water fountain for a drink. "Remember to watch," he said, an index finger banging his chest. He decided he needed to be more specific, and concluded with, "Only me!"

Meanwhile, Hallel was absorbed in her practice. Her lips moved as she told herself what she needed to do, memorizing the moves with her body and mind. When Bob came over to teach her something new, her face froze in solemn concentration as she listened to his words and committed the movements of his hands and feet to memory. She imitated him deliberately and carefully. When, serendipitously, her eyes caught mine, she became animated and unabashedly directed me to watch her.

Behind the glass wall, the children went through established motions, submitting themselves to the decree of this teacher and his art. They could see their efforts and progress through the mirrored wall and through my approving glance. It was as close to perfect as I ever got in meeting their needs. My proud glance created by decree, "Feel good about yourself."

Kee tov. It is good.

But decree only went so far. God did not create human beings by fiat, but through relationship. God blew divine breath into our lungs and souls, a life that itself could create life. When an hour was up, decree vanished and relationship reinstated itself. I dreaded it. The kids came pouring into the halls, rummaging through cubbies and shelves, leaving behind the open space with the hardwood floor, white walls, and clear expectations. We looked for scattered shoes, and stuffed clothes into canvas bags. I grumbled about a missing sock. The clarity of the Energy Arts Studio rapidly dissipated as we made our way to the parking lot and passed the snack machines. *Can I have an ice cream? A dollar? I want chips. You said next time we could get it.*

Yosef met us at the JCC to have dinner together and take the four kids to the girls' school. His work—a multimedia nonprofit he had founded, focused on Jewish education and social justice—was just a few blocks away. The plan was for him to take Hallel to get ready for her choir performance. I would take an hour to exercise on the running machines and meet them at the school in time for the concert. Aliza asked if she could go rock climbing in the gym, but there wasn't time.

We got to the front of the building and realized Aliza wasn't with us. She must have gone to the gym anyway. Yosef went back, but the rock-climbing wall was closed. He looked around the gym and exercise rooms while I checked the bathrooms.

Yosef, angry, decided to go on ahead with the other kids. Hallel didn't want to leave Aliza behind, but we harangued her toward the car. Near the front door of the JCC sat Alla, a Russian immigrant who had been both Hallel and Adari's loving preschool teacher. We passed before her like a parade of highlights from family court. Yosef dragged Hallel with deranged determination and a hard-set mouth. I whiningly demanded that a kvetching Adari get away from the snack machine. Even in the midst of this humiliating scene, I smiled knowingly at Alla, rolling my eyes in mock exasperation, conveying: *I'm in control, despite how it looks. I know what I'm doing, and I'm sticking to my maternal guns.*

Yosef took three kids in the minivan and left me his car. By the time I found Aliza I was furious, checking my watch repeatedly for effect. What effect it had I'm not sure. Love child of Maxwell Smart and the Rain Man? I accused her of selfishness and blamed her for my having to miss exercising, "which the doctor said I need." She was silent.

As I battered my words at her, I knew part of my anger was at Yosef for storming away, and part was at Aliza for fulfilling my own resistance to exercising. "Am I not allowed an hour to myself to go to the gym? Do you have to have everything you want when you want it?"

"You said that already," Aliza mumbled from the back seat, where she sat "to keep away" from me.

"I guess it's my fault, then," I said. "I spoiled you."

Silence.

"If we hurry we can still get to school in time for the concert."

"I'm not going," she said.

"I really wanted to see the Hanukkah performance, but you don't care," I said.

It was 6:30 p.m. and winter dark. The street lamps cast tight white circles, as if the particles of light had to huddle together for warmth. As I turned left, Aliza finally broke her silence. "I want to die," she said, and opened the door as if to jump from the moving car.

I swerved to the side of the road, thinking, "I am going to slap her across the face." And I did—hard.

She struggled to look unfazed.

"NEVER do that again!" I shouted.

"I couldn't help it," she said. "I can't control myself."

I was scared and drove home slowly, the doors locked, watching her in the rearview mirror. At home she lay on her bed and I busied myself with household chores, occasionally jotting down thoughts to share with her therapist.

Yosef brought the other kids home and we got them to bed. Adar and Ashira fell right to sleep exhausted. I lay on Hallel's bed with her to hear about the concert and try to put a loving end to a discordant evening. She was in the mood to share some intimate thoughts with me, so I devoted my attention to her, even though my anxiety pulled me to Aliza, who had been alone in her room since we got home.

Hallel spoke quietly. "Mama, I want to tell you something, okay? When you or Abba say goodnight and leave my room and close the door, I talk out loud to God. I told God that I don't think that Bin Laden or Saddam Hussein should die for what they did, but that I know my family doesn't agree with me. I asked God if I was right in not wanting them to be killed for what they did, and to tell me in a dream. But She never did. I asked if She ever sleeps and to let me know in a dream, but I didn't get an answer to that either."

I told her that Jewish tradition teaches that God "neither slumbers nor sleeps."

"But that's just a myth," she said. "How do you know if it's really true?"

Perhaps Hallel felt that Yosef and I had slumbered—had failed to protect and meet the needs of our children. She knew that Adari's birth parents had disappeared from his life. Did she think that Yosef would really leave her behind? Parenting by decree—"Aliza, get in the car now"—didn't work. Engaging in relationship was messy, painful and uncertain.

"Also," Hallel continued, "I asked God to help Aliza. She's in fifth grade now and when she gets homework she doesn't do it all, and then the next day she has even more. Next year she's gonna be in sixth grade and she's gonna have even more homework and then she'll have a pile this high, so I asked Adonai to help her. Don't tell any of my friends what I said, especially not Leah because she's not good at keeping secrets. They might say, *You talk to AIR? It's just AIR."* She paused. "Do you think God listens to me?"

Lying next to her in the dark room, I whispered, "I am so proud of you that you talk to God. It's so beautiful that you do that, sweetie." Pride seemed so objective. I was *moved* by her—her sincerity, her pure love, her *cholat nefesh*, a soul's yearning for God. A homesickness for one's divine parent. She longed to know what was good and right. "Abba and I knew what we were doing when we named you Hallel Ma'ayan."

"Praise God?"

"Yes, Hallel is praise for God. And Ma'ayan is a wellspring, a symbol for Torah. A well nourishes the body the way Torah nourishes the soul."

"Last year in second grade the teachers told us to draw a picture of Moses and God talking. Me and Leah didn't know how to draw God. So we made symbols, like a crown. How would *you* draw God?"

"I might have drawn lines that symbolize a voice, because God creates with words," I said. "But I love the way you did it. I love that you used symbols. That was so smart."

I scratched her back, and together we sang *Shema*, the nightly Hebrew prayer.

Shema Yisrael, Adonai Eloheinu, Adonai Echad.

Hear O Israel, Adonai is our God, Adonai is One.

V'ahavta et Adonai elohecha . . . You shall love Adonai your God with all your heart, with all your soul, and with all your strength.

Lying there with Hallel I felt power in every word whispered. The low voices added to the intensity of the evening's drama. I sensed that at this moment, in a more defined way than at other times, I was creating Hallel's reality through listening to her, as well as through the words I chose.

As I left her room, I set her CD player to repeat one song: *Hashiveinu Adonai*. Lay me down, oh God, to rest, and raise me up to life renewed.

I took a deep breath and knocked on Aliza's door. I was ready to be with her calmly. Aliza lay on her side, staring, thinking, and I lay down next to her. Somehow, in the past hour or so, she had moved from angry to reflective to sad. In the quiet of her room, the agonies that had been lurking in her fifth-grade life began to take shape. Out of the quiet she began to talk: about her friends at school, and how mean some kids can be. She talked about girls snapping at her. She said that she and Elan used to be the best basketball players, "but now it's Elan and Talia." She said she liked her teacher, Lucy, but didn't want to be seen as teacher's pet, so she told the kids that I said I'd buy her four Game Boy games if she were nice to the teachers. She asked if I would really buy them for her. "No, but it's fine to say that if it helps."

I was so happy and relieved that we had bought her a new bed. She was never fully comfortable on her old mattress. This one was softer. After her first night in it, she awoke with a grin. "We'd better return it," she said. "We'll complain to the manager that the bed's too comfortable and now I don't want to get out of it in the morning."

We were quiet, and then I sang *Shema*, rubbing her feet as she sank into sleep.

I wanted her to love herself the way I loved her when I was at my best.

Chapter 21

Time to Come

I took on redecorating with a messianic fervor, as if I could rec-reate Eden for my family if I chose the right paints and rugs. I plastered, sandpapered, and painted the kids' bedrooms. I got lost in the color chips in the Home Depot paint department, visualizing our walls coated in sea foam green and purple. Laura—living with us a week a month from L.A. because she was working as the voice of Laura, the secretary, on the animated series *Dr. Katz: Professional Therapist*—was my design guru.

A fantasy tape played in my mind of my family living in these renewed spaces—happy, enterprising, organized. As I worked with imagination, color, and texture to create the right balance of contrast and harmony, serenity and stimulation, I imagined our home like the cross section of a dollhouse, my children in their rooms pursuing their individual passions, excelling in their academic work, and in harmony with their parents and siblings.

Aliza's academic troubles and social angst would melt away in her cozy but liberatingly organized new room that once was Adar's.

We painted two walls a deep blue called "Cast a Spell," and on the other two, shades of light blue, a billowy sky effect, surrounding the large leafy tree my mother had painted for Adar over four years earlier. The apples hanging from the branches were always fresh and red, the birds in the trees always singing, and the eggs—four of them now, one for each child—peacefully nested in their strong round roost.

In my imagination I conjured a new school desk for Aliza with a cup of steaming tea to the upper right of a textbook. Beside the desk stands a bookshelf with her schoolwork filed, even color-coded, and not under a seat in the van alongside an oozing brown lunch bag from the previous summer.

Hallel's erratic temper and angry outbursts faded into the psychedelic relaxation of the space I was painting—purple-y blue on the low walls, off-white on the gabled attic ceiling. Her room on the third floor would be the perfect home for her lava lamps and disco ball. Homework would be set neatly beside a mug of sharpened pencils. Oh, look! There I am bringing her a cup of hot chocolate. (Wow, I've really lost weight!)

Adar and the next child we would adopt would laugh and play in the big bedroom. (If there's anything more gratifying than idealizing your kids in fantasy, it's idealizing a child you haven't even met yet.) Trucks and cars make tracks around the woven oval rug of lavenders and blues. The purple walls and fire engine–red shelves provide just the right balance of safe haven and fun. The beds are far enough apart to allow for individual bedtime stories and songs, but close enough for them to whisper later in the dark. I'd be feather-dusting the mantel while all that family perfection hummed and whirred around me.

It was easy to connect these visions with the Jewish idea of *olam ha'ba*. This "time to come" is our tradition's fantasy, born of our longing for a perfected world of universal peace, social justice, safety and health. Generations of rabbis have outlined many versions of what this ideal universe will look like, although as far as I know none has involved lava lamps and disco balls. They do, though, have elements in common with my fantasy family, such as peace, health, beautiful surroundings, meaningful lives, and diversity. Creating a family of mixed skin colors is a result of my earliest imaginings about the world and about my someday family.

The rabbis describe a world with no more anguish or death; illumination the world over; destroyed cities rebuilt; healing waters flowing from Jerusalem; all creatures, even animals, living in covenant with God; rivers of wine, honey, milk and balsam; and winds bringing the scent of spices from the Garden of Eden.

Just as there are hundreds of images associated with *olam ha'ba*, there are many paths to this messianic time. One is human endeavor efforts toward social justice and peace, acts of loving-kindness, patience, wisdom, and learning. It's a goal, an ideal, toward which each of us must labor. It's in our hands.

Another version is more passive, awaiting the arrival of a messiah, or messenger, to herald a divine transformation. These messiahs also take many forms in the Jewish imagination, from prophets to paupers. Therefore, it is taught, anyone might be the Messiah, so don't be a schmuck.

Sometimes I sent our babysitter to collect the kids from school so I could keep painting. Transforming their bedrooms was more satisfying than actual parenting. I followed clear, concrete steps—with scope for color and creativity—to a predictable, mapped, co-ordinated, desired outcome.

Raising children is messy, muddled, and often loud. I never knew who started the fight or needed a hug or a reprimand. Was Aliza just taking time alone, or retreating in a reclusive, debilitating way? Was

Hallel's anger justified? Irrational? Both? Were they watching too many DVDs, or were they taking needed downtime? Was Adari experiencing real pain (adoption-related, maybe?) or just pissed because I didn't buy him a Bob the Builder gadget? And who was the culprit who smeared oatmeal on the rug?

The parenting I did in my mind—the messianic vision—was much more gratifying than actual engagement with live children, although the new room arrangements were real enough. Only Adari got cold feet about leaving the room he'd had since he was a baby. He protested on the first night in his new room, looking up at the painted stars that had recently glowed above his sisters as they fell asleep. "I hate my new room. I want my old one," he hissed, eyes narrowed. "I am not going to sleep here. I hate this room and I hate you."

I lay down with him and held him tight, saying to myself, "I am going to hold him down until he is asleep. That is how I am handling this. No second guesses." I comforted myself with my conviction. I told him stories about Little Mouse—a character he and I had created together (Little Mouse had become very angry with Mama Mouse)—and about what Bob the Builder and his friends fixed together. I sang to him. It placated him intermittently, but his hostility returned and prevailed. When I finished singing "Puff, the Magic Dragon," Adar offered his own rendition: *Puff the magic steamroller ran over mommy until she was dead. And this is for real.*

I had spent so much time immersed in house projects—my castle-creating—that I didn't have the usual scaffolding on which to stand with Adar. When I spent less time with my kids, engagement with them became more formidable, relationships more tentative.

The next day, I tore myself away from my paints and dreams and picked up Adari from preschool after lunch. With two hours to ourselves before Aliza and Hallel came home, we drove to the Charles River, where I unloaded his bike near the fenced-in playground. "Do you want to play here for a while?" I asked.

"No," he said, walking his bike past the stretch of gate to our left, his eyes straight ahead. "Maybe another time when there's not a dog."

I searched the play area and finally located the threat, all ten fluffy pounds of it, on a leash in the corner. I laughed with pride at Adar's ability to see everything at once.

The sky's clear, pale blue complemented the deeper hue of the river. I had learned this lingo—*complement, contrast, blend*—in choosing paint colors under the guidance of the guy from Home Depot. To my delight, on this warming spring day, I was completely immersed in a different kind of creation—strengthening the threads of relationship with my son. I was focused on him and our walk, not distressed and distracted by my own boredom (epitomized by how many of the girls' plays and skits I attended where I sat in the audience of two, feigning enthusiasm while stealing long looks at the newspaper spread at my feet).

The familiar longing for something beyond the parent-child dyad had melted away into satisfaction in our adventure together. Adar rode and I walked along the smooth, paved riverside path. On both sides were large trees with long, thick branches stretching and bending, perfect for climbing.

The joy in my surroundings reminded me of another rabbinic interpretation of *olam ha'ba*. "The Holy One will bring forth from the Holy of Holies (the sacred ark of the ancient Temple in Jerusalem) a stream along whose sides will grow all manner of precious fruits."

Instead of immersing myself in projects to avoid the complexity of raising children, I resolved to carve out more non-fraught moments like this one. I would construct scaffolding made of time and positive interactions, and nurture the trees' precious fruits—the lives of my children. Messianic moments would co-exist with, and give hope to, our complicated lives.

We came to a bridge with no side rails. The river was to our left, the grass to our right. It was wide, not risky to cross, but Adari rode his bike slowly to my right, protected from the water.

"What would you do if I fell in?" he asked, his brow furrowed.

"Oh, sweetie, you won't!"

"But what if I *do*?"

"I would jump in and save you," I assured him.

"Would you be able to save me?"

"Absolutely."

"How do you know?"

"Because when a child is in trouble his mother gets superhuman strength." As I said that, I thought, I'm an idiot. What if someday I am unable to save him from danger? Children are injured all the time, and it's rarely the fault of their mothers. What about Adar's birth mother? Did she fail him? In my desire to prove myself irrevocably, viscerally, Adar's mother, I had lied. And he knew it.

Back on the path, there were little rotaries around patches of bright green grass. Grinning at me as he checked on my progress, Adari circled each one until I caught up. I watched him ride, so masterful on his red two-wheeler, his blue metallic helmet shimmering in the sunlight. The path was full of people reveling in the winter-free day—young men and women on bikes and roller blades, elderly people walking arm in arm, mothers and fathers pushing strollers. As we walked, I watched endless ripples form and disappear in the river's flow, each one a hopeful reach to the cloudless sky.

Cambridge has always made me feel full of possibility. Across the river, its skyline stood tall—Harvard, hotels, research companies, MIT—a city with people from many lands. Great minds, new immigrants, and Mayflower descendants. The sun, high and gold, highlighted the stretch of gray buildings with a silver lining.

On a dock in front of the skyline stood young adults, probably Harvard students, in colorful shirts. Canoes and a few sailboats with bright, multicolored sails surrounded them, as if applauding their youth and potential. I felt happy and whole walking along the riverside, enjoying the river and the trees and the sky and my son. I noticed with satisfaction that I didn't feel old, fat, and underachieving when I saw the slim coeds in their shorts and belly-shirts on the dock across the river, exuding an intense, anything-is-possible sexual energy that I would probably never know again.

Riding before me, Adar seemed like such a big boy on his red two-wheeler. Gone was the small blue bike with the wobbly training wheels. A tall man on a high, sleek bicycle came from behind us and passed to the left, making Adar seem suddenly tiny again. Unexpected forces can change our perceptions of the world; they can harm or save, enrich or diminish, embrace or expel our children. There is so much I cannot do to make a safe, perfect world for this child, who didn't feel dwarfed at all by the tall figure riding past him. He continued to pedal quickly, steadily, a union of body and mind.

I framed the shot of Adar as he pedaled away between leafy trees and river until he was at just the right distance to create the illusion that I held him in my hands.

My daughters were the only white children at the Jewish Multiracial Network annual retreat in the spring of 2001. The other kids were Asian and Latino, or brown like their two-and-a-half-year-old brother. The retreat offered great activities, thought-provoking workshops, a beautiful campus, and heart-breakingly beautiful scenes of children of many colors clapping hands and singing *bim bam Shabbat shalom*.

The majority of the participants were sincere seekers—excited to be with other Jewish families. But a few were energized by resentment—the easily offended how-dare-you set. And they pissed me off. They gave me reason to be an easily offended how-dare-you rabbi.

A mother during group session: "I refuse to convert my child. That's just racism."

Me in my head: *No, it would be racism if every generation had to convert anew.*

Mother: "You just wait, your family is a temple's worst nightmare."

Me: *Maybe you are.*

Mother: "You ask your white Jewish friends, none of them would let their daughters marry your son."

Me: *Maybe it's YOUR kids they don't want in their lives.*

(When I checked that question with my friend Sara, she assured me that she would be honored if her son married Adar!)

I was being a bitch because I had no place to stand in the world. It had been five years since I had been the rabbi of a congregation. The book Yosef and I wrote together, *Jewish Family & Life*, had given me some professional status for a few years—book tours, media, teaching. But that was done, too. I had nothing to offer at the retreat. I just wanted to go hide in our cabin each evening until it was time to go home.

After the retreat, I got a call from a nice woman I had met there. I had taken some woodsy walks with Audrey, a former dancer in rock-hard shape. She had no bones to pick. She and her husband, Paul, had met in their thirties and were at the retreat in anticipation of their baby son's arrival from Korea. Now that he was here, would I do the baby-naming?

I was honored and happy they had asked me. But I couldn't even think. It was the end of the school year, with its parent-teacher conferences and performances and ceremonies, and I hadn't even arranged camp for the kids or figured out our travel plans.

"We're so excited, we want to do something as soon as possible, even if it means our distant family can't come," said Audrey.

"Maybe you want to consider, though, holding off so it can include everyone?" I suggested, searching through the mess on the counter for my calendar in case she really wanted to make a date now.

"Really?" she said. "You think it's worth waiting?"

"Well, he's past eight days old, anyway. Why don't you do the circumcision and *mikveh* immersion first, and have a ceremony in the fall when everyone can make it?"

"Okay," she said. "I'll talk to Paul, and we'll contact you after the summer to make a date."

Early on September 11, 2001, a giant dumpster and truck pulled up in the driveway behind our house. I had been cleaning up the basement, clearing the way for good energy in the world. Hooray! All the junk that Yosef and I had accumulated over the years and that grew in the basement like fungus was on its way out. New possibilities for spiritual, emotional, and intellectual growth were just around the corner.

I drove the kids to school, and on the drive home NPR cut to breaking news. A plane had just flown into one of the Twin Towers.

At home, the men who had come to help remove the stuff from my basement were in the living room watching a small black-and-white TV that rested on a chair. They were watching a man leap to his death from the burning height of the tower—over and over as the video replayed.

The black hole of destruction-in-an-instant sucked normal life into its vortex. I called Yosef and insisted he come home right away. I would go get the kids early. "I can't," he said. "We're putting out an immediate issue on talking to children about tragedy."

"Oh good, that will comfort your children as they huddle without you, and the nuclear waste kills us off one by one."

"If you want to get Adar, fine. He's little enough that it won't scare him. But please don't get the girls early from school," he pleaded.

I picked up Adar from day care. He ran to me, and I pulled him in for a long hug. He rested his cheek on my shoulder, and I kissed his warm neck, which smelled like Play-Doh and was rough with sand. His breath smelled like cookies—buttery and sugary and vanilla—and his long hair, an exploding corkscrew garden, tickled my cheek. Teachers whispered in twos and threes on the periphery of the playground, children screeched and rode in plastic cars, but they all receded into a hazy background as I whispered in Adar's ear: "I missed you so much today." I felt like I was speaking for his birth mother, too.

The next week, a friend from the Jewish Multiracial Network called, sobbing. "Susan, Paul was on one of those planes. Poor Audrey, and that sweet baby boy they just adopted from Korea."

Part 3

Chapter 22

The Moment Waits for You

For me, adopting another child had little to do with practical-ity. Did we have the money for another adoption? No, we would remortgage our house. Did we have enough time so that each child was fully ready for school each day, with sneakers that fit and three decent meals a day? Breakfast was any food that wouldn't spill if the minivan hit a bump, and socks were *just fine* for gym class.

We weren't talking about adopting a child from some fancy-pants-eat-your-breakfast-like-a-mensch family. We'd be adopting a child from an orphanage in a very poor country. We were enough for a child to have a good life, a real family. An American mother I met in Ethiopia with six kids already and adopting three older ones from Adar's orphanage said, "We might have rice and beans for dinner, but we have three more smiling faces at the table."

As vegetarians, we often had rice and beans for dinner anyway, or bright orange mac-and-cheese from a box. With another adop-tion, we might have more debt, lose the Jewish day school option, reduce one-on-one time with each kid by one-fifth, and make do without a summer vacation, but in return, a child would get a chance at a life with parents and siblings, and get taken out of the pool of candidates for the drug, war, and sex trades. My heart's response to my brain's doubts was twofold: One, if my children were ever at risk, wouldn't I want loving parents to take a chance on them? Two, if it's the right thing to do, why suffer over it? It was a case of "do the right thing, pray, and spend money on therapists."

I prayed a lot. I prayed every time the phone rang that it wasn't the nurse saying Aliza was asleep in her office or a teacher saying Hallel had run away from class.

My prayers were not answered.

Lucy, the head of the girls' middle school, called us in for a meeting about Aliza's extreme disorganization and Hallel's temper tantrums. Hallel was in a Monday evening "social skills cooking class," where they mostly sugared up the kids they were trying to contain. They made cakes layered with frosting that was further layered with gummy bears, M&M's, and sprinkles.

Hallel was happy to be in a group where she was the relatively functional one. "The girl next to me licked my arm," she reported. The teachers emailed a report on the new skill of the week. "Today we learned about 'bubble thoughts.' Things we think, but put away in a bubble and don't say." My sisters couldn't wait to read the latest installment, which I forwarded immediately. "I need a class like that!" said Laura. They practiced using and reading facial expressions, making eye contact, and monitoring their own and other people's body language. They practiced switching topics, taking turns, making pleasantries, and identifying and appreciating other people's perspectives.

Also important for Hallel, they learned to modulate volume. The child had a very high volume.

"I wonder if this is really the time to adopt another child," Lucy said.

"Another adoption is Susan's dream, so it's mine, too," Yosef told her.

"Good boy," I said.

"Woof."

Today, Lucy was telling us to take Hallel home for punching someone in the face. Who was it this time? Daniel, the son of my sister-close friend Sharon.

"You *hit* him, Hallel? In the *face*?"

"He was really annoying."

"Punching someone in the head is not appreciating his perspective," I reminded her.

When I went to pick up Aliza later that day, Sharon stopped me in the hallway. "Oh, honey, I'm so sorry Hallel got suspended," she said.

"Um, Sharon. She punched Daniel in the face."

"I'm sure he irritated her."

The school said Hallel could come back when they felt she would no longer run away from class or hit anyone. How was I supposed to fix her and get her back to school? I'd need an academic schedule to keep up with her schoolwork. More therapy sessions, although we were already paying for those with checks from a credit card that was regularly being refused at the market. How could I get my child what she needed? And Aliza was miserable. She wanted to escape the confines of the small Jewish day school and find a place where she could grow in her own way. She wouldn't even brush her hair until her teacher threatened to cut it. She was moving ever inward, into her imagination and books. I was lost, and my compass was somewhere under a load of crap.

Sometimes there's a Sinaitic current in my life, clarity of purpose. Sometimes there's not. My spiritual antennae get varying levels of reception along life's road, and there are times when I feel a
bit lost. What is the human purpose again? What is a Jew's role, as
God's partner, in making the world better? What am I good at that
I can bring to the effort? And where's Aliza's backpack?

On the road to adoption, I always get a good, clear signal from
the radio towers on Sinai. With Adar, I thought there was a child
who pre-existed Yosef and me, one child that was meant for us the
way the rabbis teach that God determines one's *besheirt*, your one
true love, even before you are born. The way Plato thought that
perfect beauty existed and that we could uncover it through
thought and reason. A spiritual journey would bring me to my
pre-destined child.

As destined-to-be-ours as Adar felt, that's not really the way it
worked. Yosef and I had placed ourselves within a tradition, used
its tools, and created a path that led to a child who became ours.
Not so different from the daughters we conceived. This adoption
road, too, would be paved-as-we-go by the tools of our lives: values, family, instincts, passions, Jewish rhythms, and a clear set of
instructions from the agency.

While we planned our second adoption, Yosef read a book on
the Jews of India reclaiming their roots and slowly moving to Israel. These "lost Jews," many of whom were just discovering their
origins, lived in a region with many orphans. "A child can have a
double homecoming—to his new family and to Judaism," Yosef
said.

"But it's really hard for non-Indians to adopt from India," I
pointed out.

"Let's try for a few months," he said. "I like the idea of shades of
color in our family, like a rainbow."

"What are you, *gay*?"

We engaged an agency that facilitated adoptions from many countries, because adopting from India was difficult and slow and we wanted other readily available options if necessary. There was a caste system for potential adoptive parents: Indians in India, Indians outside of India, one Indian parent, all the way down to non-Indian parents. From there, parents with two or fewer children had priority. We were at the very bottom of the heterosexual barrel. Despite the millions of orphans who would not get families, our chances of becoming the parents of one were minuscule. Even after our application was complete it took months before we received a referral, the only one we could expect for a long time.

I collected the packet from the post office and opened it in the car. It was a little boy, five years old. On the top of the pile was a head shot, as if he were applying for a modeling job with Feed the Children. At home, Yosef and I read the file, looked at the boy's picture, and researched his medical and developmental issues on the Web.

"He's not ours," I said. I don't know why I thought that—or, rather, felt it. And it killed me. I wanted this to be our child. I wanted this child to call somebody Mommy. But it wouldn't be me.

"Ethiopia?" I asked.

"Ethiopia," Yosef said.

Because the odds of adopting from India had not been in our (or the children's) favor, the agency had said we could switch our file to Ethiopia and not lose time. We had a personal timetable to complete the adoption process: one year.

Each of our children's names is a verb that describes an act before God: Aliza, *rejoice.* Hallel, *praise.* Adar, *exalt.* That was not planned. I only realized the pattern when looking for a name for

Ashira. I kept coming back to a line in the prayer book: *Ashira l'adonai, kee gao ga'ah.* I will sing before God, for God is a redeemer. Ashira, *sing.* Use your voice to sing a better world into reality. And it dawned on me that all our kids' names were action words.

"Earlier generations, who were able to make use of the Holy Spirit through prophets, named their children for events that were to occur," teaches the Talmud. "Whereas we, who are unable to make use of the Holy Spirit, name our children after our immediate forebears."

Screw that. Yosef and I would make use of the Holy Spirit. We would be co-creators of those "events that were to occur." One of the quotations outlining one of the seven gates of the Old City that surrounded the text on our *ketuba*, our marriage contract, is *l'takein olam b'malkhut shadai,* "to repair the world within God's sovereignty." Through naming, we use language to pray and to create.

For months before the second adoption, I thumbed through Hebrew prayer books for a name for our son-to-be. Again, a certain line called to me: *Tov l'hodot la'adonai, ul'zamer l'shimcha elyon.* It is good to give thanks to God, to sing Your praise, Exalted One.

Zamir. *To sing God's praises.*

If I introduced my kids by their names in English, you would be forgiven for thinking they were peppy members of a born-again Jesus band. "These are my little blessings: Rejoice, Praise, Exalt, Sing Out, and Sing It."

Now we just needed to find little Sing It.

Showtime. There was a package from the adoption agency in my mailbox.

I summoned my friends to duty. Sue and Judy followed me into the darkened living room, where I had set up a television screen and DVD player on the mantel over the fireplace. There were two

DVDs in the package, "September" and "October." They both featured children at the orphanage who were waiting for homes. I could wait for "November," due to arrive in another two weeks, but no, I was going to choose now. I wanted the weight of choice lifted. I wanted pictures of our new child I could show to everyone. I wanted to order those really fun return-address labels with cartoon pictures of Yosef, our five children, and me.

I aimed the remote control and pressed play.

Judy and Sue sat in two of the three silvery-gray felt-covered armchairs that I had set in a row for this viewing. They left me the middle seat so that I'd have a friend on either side. The armchairs had belonged to my mother's mother, Goldie. Her living room had been all white except for these chairs and a shiny silvery couch, which I had also kept. My aunt always said that my grandmother's house looked like the inside of a refrigerator.

What would Goldie have thought of the three of us holding hands across the arms of her chairs, watching DVDs of Ethiopian orphans? She had spent her life trying to overcome the humiliation of her Polish accent and childhood poverty. By the time I knew her, my grandmother spoke English like an American queen—every syllable cut and polished like a diamond.

"Okay," I instructed my friends. "Focus mostly, but maybe not exclusively, on boys younger than Adari and older than Ashira. The three-, four-, and five-year-olds."

"September" opened on a boy who looked about eleven. Gail, the director of the orphanage and the video's unseen narrator, described the scenario: *Here we have Johannes. He is thirteen years old and has been at Wanna House for a year. He loves sports. Do you love to play soccer, Johannes?* Johannes smiled and nodded. *Wonderful!*

Gail's voice was high-pitched and singsongy. It reminded me of Snow White singing to her echo in a well: *I'm wishing (I'm wishing) for the one I love (for the one I love) to find me (to find me) today (today).*

There was a montage of dozens of babies. With each close-up, Gail recited a tiny biography. *Found by police and brought to us three weeks ago. Appears healthy. Grandfather brought her in at five days old. Mother died in childbirth.* There were a surprising number of twins.

The older children had been recorded individually, unless they had siblings. They took turns sitting on or standing by a bench, their backs to the blank slate of a white wall. The only hint of outdoor surroundings was the play of shadow behind them as they either fidgeted or stayed still as a chalk outline, staring deerlike into the camera.

Gail asked questions in simple English, and the children replied with nods and smiles. Probably none of them spoke English at all, but the video made it appear that they understood. Maybe the technique rendered them less formidable to potential parents.

Now we have Kassa, Desta, and Yonas. Kassa is fourteen, Desta is eleven, and Yonas is four. They are siblings who just came to us last month. Their mother died and their father is sick. The oldest boy looked down, the middle one smiled, and the youngest squirmed and glanced up shyly at his brothers. *They look out for each other and get along well with the other children here.*

By the end of the second disc, "October," the three of us had identified seven possibilities, simply by using the objective criteria of age and gender.

"Yosef and I will adopt one of these boys," I said with certainty, but by the time my friends were at the front door putting on their jackets, I was fishing for reassurance. "Maybe I'm just being impatient and should wait to see November's disc," I said. "Maybe then a child will leap off the screen, and it will be obvious."

Sue placed her hand on my arm. "Let's see what Yosef says when you show him these seven," she suggested. "Something might be clear to him, honey."

"He's got good instincts," added Judy, kissing me on the cheek.

When Yosef got home, we sat on the silvery-gray armchairs. On the precipice of finding our fifth and final child, I held a remote control in my left hand, and my husband's hand with my right. "Just show me the seven," he said. It was too painful to watch the presentation of all these children whose shy smiles were seasoned with loss and longing.

I fast-forwarded to each little boy, using the list of location numbers I had written on the back of an envelope—four-year-old Yihune was 3 minutes, 8 seconds in. Five-year-old Tefere was 10 minutes, 51 seconds in. The fifth of these seven children (28 minutes, 14 seconds) was a little boy who was sitting and smiling— slyly? mischievously?—while sometimes glancing off-camera to his right.

"This is Kedir Ismael," came Gail's singsong. "But we call him Gideon. He's three-and-a-half years old. He's from Dessa, and he's been here at Wanna House for three months. You can see he's got a bandage above his left eye. That's because he got into a little scrape with one of the other children this morning."

"That's our kid," Yosef said, deadpan.

Yosef could move forward like this, while most of us stumble on our own fear. Even Moses was said to have hesitated at the yet-to-part Sea of Reeds (Red Sea) and then again at thunderous Sinai. Finally in both places God called to him, saying, "The moment waits for you." Yosef seemed to know that instinctively.

My father, the sworn atheist, would later say, with genuine contemplation, "Do you think God caused him to get into a fight and cut his forehead so you'd find him?"

Who knows? Of all the children in the whole world, here was ours. It's how the rabbis describe God's choice of the Holy Temple in Jerusalem. Revelation could have happened anywhere, the rabbis teach, but after God chose the Land of Israel, all other lands were eliminated. All of Israel could have sufficed, but God chose Jerusalem. All of Jerusalem could have served as Divine Central, but God singled out the Temple.

We had settled on a country, Ethiopia, at which point all other lands were eliminated. Then we settled on an orphanage, after which all other orphanages were eliminated. Then we settled on a child, and all other children were eliminated. I called the adoption agency and claimed the boy they called Gideon, but who had originally been named Kedir.

Unlike with Adar, we received information about Kedir's birth mother. She was a day laborer named Yafete who had died of AIDS, probably while giving birth. The only thing recorded about the father was that he too died of AIDS. Yafete had received assistance from a health organization serving her rural village—including medication that probably saved the baby's life. Her sister had taken care of the orphaned infant until he was almost a year old, and then asked the same organization to take him. They placed him at A-Hope, an AIDS orphanage in Addis Ababa. He lived there two and a half years before he and seventeen of the other children were found to be HIV negative, and then moved to Wanna House, where he became available for adoption.

We sent Kedir Ismael-Gideon a T-shirt, as per the agency's instructions. At the orphanage, wearing an unfamiliar shirt alerted the other children that you would soon leave to join a family. We were also told to send a picture album. My mother took pictures of all of us in different parts of the house, to show Kedir his new family and home.

Adar panicked. "He won't be my brother. I won't talk to him," he whined, arms crossed, eyebrows slanted up sharply toward his nose. We sent the pictures in which Adar looked the least demonic.

What happened to "I want a brown brother?"

Sigal, Adari's first-grade teacher, made some magic. She pasted a picture of Kedir—who we already called Zamir—onto a big sheet of cardboard, and held it up in class at circle time. She asked each child to say how they might feel if they were getting a new brother or sister. "Excited." "Worried." "Happy." "Scared." "Confused." "Jealous." "Proud." Then each child dictated specific wishes for Adar, and Sigal wrote them on the cardboard around the picture. *I hope that you and your brother have fun together. I hope that your new brother likes his new house. I hope he plays cars with you. I hope you can teach him a lot of things.*

Kedir (in Hebrew, *kadar*) means pottery. There are many rabbinic references to God as Potter and humanity as the vessel God created, but Yosef and I rejected that metaphor for our new son, and for our family as a whole. Until now, by necessity, this child had been like pottery, shaped by the loving hands of God—the care of an aunt, the help of a charity organization, the tending of an orphanage. But with a shift of only two Hebrew letters, his new name, Zamir, which rhymed with his old name, would symbolize his transformation from product to actor, from passive vessel to singer of his own song.

Chapter 23

The Music of the City

I was about to board a plane to Ethiopia with Aliza, almost thirteen, and Hallel, who had just turned eleven. They were joining me on this trip thanks to a dear friend who had given us all his airline points so the girls could share this experience. "I hate my job, but if all my work travel enables Aliza and Hallel to go meet their new brother, I'll feel like it's been worth it," he said.

I, in turn, was grateful that I would only have to leave three people, not five. I was more worried about Yosef's twenty-minute ride back on the Mass Pike than I was about our flight. If Yosef, Adar, and Ashira were killed, would we find out before we boarded? Would the terrible news reach us in Addis Ababa? "Call my cell phone when you get back to the house," I instructed Yosef.

Adar wrapped himself around my leg and cried, "Don't go, Mama! Stay!"

"Hey Adari," Yosef said as he wheeled over a stranded luggage cart. "You want to ride this out to the sidewalk?"

As if magnetically pulled against his will, Adari loosened his hold on me and climbed onto the cart. I braced myself for Ashira's cries, but she just smiled and said, "Bye Mama, go get my new budda."

It seemed impossible that the three of us had come all the way from Newton, Massachusetts, to Addis Ababa to be paired with a skinny four-year-old whose life began in rural northern Dessa. As the sun shed its first light of the day, we thanked the appropriately named Wanna House driver and let ourselves into the guesthouse. The Muslim calls to worship rang loudly throughout the neighborhood. There was also a harsh, burning smell that made us feel sick. Our driver had explained it was from the burning bones outside the local slaughterhouse and meat processing plant, something this vegetarian did not need to know about.

It was dark in the guesthouse. Breathing the thick, throat-burning stench, redolent with images of death, we groped in the dark, unable to find a light switch or the stairs to the small second-floor apartment that had been assigned to us. Hallel became worried—maybe we weren't in the right house. We all would have preferred the Sheraton, but this guesthouse belonged to Zamir's orphanage, and I was too embarrassed to reject it for something fancy. "I'm sure it's the right place," I said. "The driver works for the orphanage. He knows." I had to embrace the unknown, be willing to feel my way in the dark. If I hadn't ventured out, heart in throat, I wouldn't have had Adar either.

We found stairs and climbed them. Then we found a lamp. Our two bedrooms and tiny salon contained flattened, worn green carpets with brown stains and frazzled edges. The green painted walls with plastic fake wood closets were worn and chipped.

I knew I would not fall asleep; that the few hours between now and when Gail came to get us would never pass.

"Hello, Susan?" A woman's voice was wafting up the stairs. It was the same singsong from the orphanage videos. "It's time to get started," she called.

Oh my God, we had overslept! I woke the girls and we rushed to get dressed and gather our things. I was not prepared, which was probably best. I could be intuitive and open, not nervously choreographed.

Gail drove us in her Jeep to the orphanage. She was a pale, blonde woman from Ontario, married to an Ethiopian man she met when he was a student in Canada. They were born-again Christians who lived outside the city in a compound for foreign evangelicals.

We walked to the right, toward a long, low building with two doors. In a room to our left were little girls tucked into their beds for a nap. On our right was the boys' room. It was small and rectangular, with four bunk beds very close together, one end pushed to the back wall and the other nearly touching the front. I watched from the doorway as Gail squeezed in front of each bunk bed. The boys were lying down, so I couldn't see their faces. I wondered at which bed she would stop, like a high-stakes game of musical beds.

At the third one she lifted a child from the top bunk. He slumped into her arms, still asleep, his head heavy on her shoulder. She walked slowly over and handed him to me.

I sat with him on the bottom of some stairs that led to a balcony above us. I held him as she had, with his head on my shoulder. Zamir lifted his head, and his weight shifted on my lap. He opened his huge brown eyes and smiled the most serene smile. Already the story I would tell him one day glimmered in my mind, the sparks of meaning.

We gazed at each other for a long time, our surroundings blurring at the corners of my vision. His eyes were like planets, huge and round. Whole worlds. Sacred mystery narrowed down to this one little boy.

The first thing we did now that Zamir was ours was to take him to the mall.

At a tchotchke store at the one fancy-ish shopping center in Addis Ababa, Zamir cried silently. His tears were oversized, perfectly formed drops. Was it about leaving the orphanage he had called home for the past year? No, he had done that with nary a backward glance. Was it the shock of a strange woman and two enthusiastic girls with long, straight, all-over-their-faces hair and thick glasses taking him away? No, he jaunted happily forward with us. This boy, who had been not-an-AIDS-orphan for less than an hour, had his arms crossed and was refusing to move, his tears streaming, because I wouldn't buy him the sunglasses he wanted.

It was my first clash with Zamir. I had already bought him a baseball cap. *Oooohhhh nooooo. I'm not going there. From day one, limits must be defined.*

I shook my head no.

At first he shrugged, which I soon learned was gesture-Amharic for "I don't accept your answer." Then the tears.

I stayed firm. Back down the escalator we found a Starbucks knock-off near the entrance to the mall. (No, they did not have soy milk. Yes, I felt like an idiot asking.) We ordered sandwiches and Mirinda orange soda for the kids. Zamir adored the soda. He finished it and indicated his desire for another.

No way. Limits from day one, Susan. Do not indulge him for fear of another meltdown. This was kid number five, and I had learned. As his face fell, but before the tears could gather in his eyes, Aliza said, "Zamir! Look what I got you!" She pulled out the sunglasses. She had surreptitiously bought them while Zamir and I stared each other down.

He put them on and smiled at me. Was he mocking me?

Back at the guesthouse, the smell of the nearby cow crematorium never eased, and every breath felt laborious and disgusting. The girls and I sat on the bed, and Zamir went to the toilet, which was just a few feet away. He kept the door open, and we watched as he sat there, his every move (movement?) fascinating to us. A stranger and totally ours. When he was done, he stood up from the toilet and touched his toes. And remained in that position. The girls and I looked at each other quizzically. Zamir kept his head down, rested his skinny fingers on his sneakers (okay, yes, new sneakers, but he really did need them), and seemed willing to hold that position indefinitely.

Suddenly I understood. *Oh my God,* I said to myself as I went into the bathroom, unrolled the toilet paper, and wiped his bottom. I shushed the girls as they cracked up. *That's how they do it at Wanna House.* There must have been a line of children during bathroom breaks waiting their turn to be wiped.

That night I lay next to Zamir on the mattress on the floor where he slept beside his sisters, who took the bunk beds. I sang *Shema* to him for the first time, followed by our family's other nightly songs: "Puff, the Magic Dragon," and "Jerusalem of Gold," with the lyrics adjusted so that the kids' names replaced some of the words. I had included Zamir since the day we chose him from the video. *Jerusalem of Aliza, and of Hallel and of Adar, of Zamir and Ashira, We are the music of the city.* As I sang I pointed to the pictures of the four siblings in his little red book, and to him, and he smiled the world's happiest smile.

Epilogue

MIKVEH

*M*oses didn't intentionally smash the tablets. He was trying
to preserve them.

The rabbis of the Talmud teach that Moses won a tug-of-war
over the tablets with God, and stood holding them in his arms.
The engraved words on the tablets themselves became furious at
the Israelites' idol worship and flew off. As they soared away, the
tablets became unbearably heavy because the words had been like
helium, buoying the tablets. Moses dropped them and they broke.

Life in suburban Boston had been wonderful in many ways. But
it had been like the tablets without words—too heavy, and missing
the kind of relationship with God that allowed for us to create as
Her partners. We hoped that our second set of tablets, buoyed by
holy text, awaited us at the foot of Sinai.

We decided to move to a kibbutz in the south of Israel.

Kibbutz Ketura was a stone's throw from Mount Sinai. The actual, original Mount Sinai. It featured simplicity: a communal dining hall for all meals, no commuting, a central laundry where you

dropped off your dirty clothes one day and picked them up clean
and folded the next. The little ones had kindergarten near where
Yosef and I worked in mud-walled, high-tech offices. The older
kids had a five-minute bus ride to the kibbutz next door, where
their grades were not permanently recorded, just used as tools for
evaluation in the learning process. It was not the imaginary Eden
my parents had wished for three decades earlier, where creation
was impossible because it was unnecessary—life was a self-enclosed
cycle in which we filled predefined roles. On this kibbutz, we
would create, grow, and change. The wide-open desert was our
new canvas.

As we readied to move to Israel, all seven of us stood together
in a *mikveh*—a Jewish ritual bath. Adar, Zamir, and Ashira were
naked, but Yosef, Aliza, Hallel, and I wore bathing suits. Yosef
and Adar had come every Friday afternoon since this progressive,
pluralistic place opened—undressing, showering, scrubbing their
feet and cleaning their nails; and then, sparkling clean, immersing
themselves in preparation for Shabbat. One role of *mikveh* is to
purify, to refresh one's soul before a holy day, and Yosef had attended *mikveh* before the Sabbath whenever possible, ever since he
had lived in Jerusalem right after college.

This *mikveh* was a much more upscale experience than the simple one Yosef had once shared with a few other religious men in
that old Jerusalem neighborhood. Here the walls and floor were a
mosaic of pale and deep gold tiles, recalling the Old City of Jerusalem alight in the evening. A long corner window allowed a rectangular ray of light to fall upon the golden hues. Wide, smooth stone
steps led in a semicircle into the pool. Adar was four when they
began this private father-son tradition, and not yet ready to dunk
his head under. Slowly, he grew comfortable with dunking his

whole body in the clear, warm water, and enjoying the small underwater lights.

When Zamir joined our family he too began to go each week.
Yosef and Adar taught him the "angels song," the slow, pensive
tune they sang together as they immersed. Now Adar took Zamir's
hand and led his new brother slowly and lovingly into these strange,
quiet waters, singing their private immersion liturgy a bit more
loudly and confidently than he had before, assuring Zamir that
lowering his body entirely into the water was nice and not scary.
Adar relished being the teacher, the knowledgeable one, in this
renewed ancient ritual.

Earlier we had met with the *beit din*—rabbinic court—made up
of three women rabbis, all dear friends, and formally affirming both
our sons' places among our people. In a way, it also affirmed our
own. Dunking in the welcoming water I asked the kids to imagine
the Sea of Reeds parting into two walls for the Israelites to pass
through to freedom, toward a covenant with God.

Two millennia after the exodus, the rabbis of the Talmud were
still arguing about the details of that episode. What did the walls of
water, created by the parting of the Sea of Reeds, look like? Clear
water with visible fish? A sprouting of thick green bushes? The
reigning opinion was ascribed to a biblical character named Serah,
the adopted daughter of Joseph's brother, Asher, the father of one
of the twelve tribes. Serah was born at the time of Joseph, but is
said to live still, playing pivotal roles in historic moments—including as a keeper of ancient knowledge. Asher had many children, but
he entrusted only Serah, his only daughter and only adopted child,
with the secret Hebrew words that would identify the eventual redeemer. When Moses approached the Israelite slaves, reporting
God's words of coming redemption, he encountered skepticism.

Why should we believe that God spoke to you? When the leaders of the people told Serah that Moses spoke the words: *Pakod Pakad'ti*, "I will surely take notice of you," she confirmed that he was, in fact, the proven redeemer. "Those are the words of redemption my great-grandfather taught my grandfather, who taught my father, who taught me."

Two thousand years after the parting of the sea, Serah interrupted the rabbis' argument about the form of the walls of water, and said, "I was there. The waters were not as you describe, but rather like lighted windows." Lighted windows, like opposing mirrors, in which each and every Jew—past, present, future—was infinitely reflected.

Now in a circle with Ashira in my arms and Zamir in Yosef's, Adar and the big girls beside us, we sang the Hebrew song that translates to: *In God's name, to my right is Micha-el, to my left is Gavri-el, before me is Uri-el, behind me is Rafa-el, and above my head,* Shechina (God's holy presence).

Serah bat Asher, Adar's foremother in Judaism and in adoption, is said to have been the only Israelite who could see angels singing above the Sea of Reeds, beyond the tall ocean walls. We, too, would look beyond the walls that both held and limited us.

The sacred waters in which the seven of us stood were, like Serah's description of the parted sea, waters of light. The boys immersed themselves, and we recited and elicited blessings both spoken and lived. Like the Sea of Reeds, this was a moment of revelation of God's renewal of a family. It would guide us to the next phase of our journey—to the foot of Mount Sinai.

The immersion complete, we were ready to climb out of the waters. Yosef paused and took my hand. We all took his cue and reached to one another as I began to sing. Yosef and the kids joined in, our voices becoming louder, more passionate, echoing like reflections of divine light.

Min ha metzar karati yah, anani bameirchav yah.

From the narrow place I call to You. God answers me from the expanse.

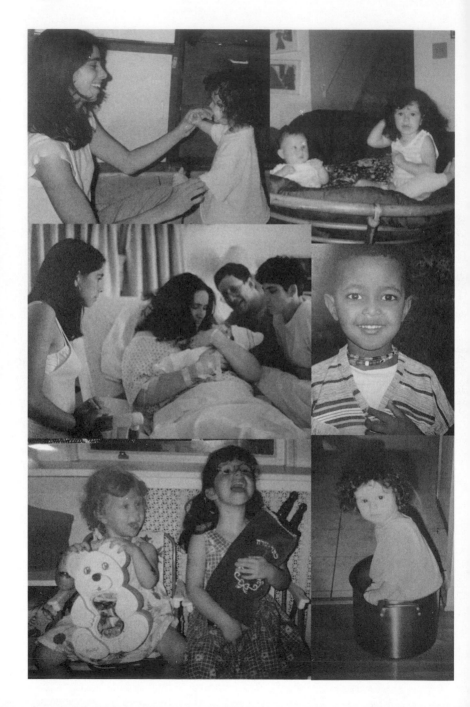

Author's Note

THE GLOBAL STATE OF ADOPTION

People—smart, well-read people—have looked at me in surprise when I say that there are tens of millions of orphans in the world. "I don't understand," they say. "It took my friends years to complete their adoption from _____." Fill in the blank— Russia, China, Romania. "I thought that parents had to wait because there are not many kids who need to be adopted."

So not. There are long waits because governments and international aid organizations such as UNICEF and Save the Children obstruct international adoption. In fact, due to self-serving policies, such organizations have caused an "international adoption cliff," reducing the number of unparented children adopted by families in the United States by two-thirds, from almost 22,991 in 2004 to 7,200 in 2013, despite tens of millions of children who do not have parents and who, vulnerable, die and are trafficked in appalling numbers.

Why? Here are some of the anti-international-adoption arguments—and my responses:

"Children have a right to their cultural heritage."

I'm not sure how you define cultural heritage, but a life of institution-alization, mental illness, sex trafficking, crime, and early death is not a worthy cultural heritage. And certainly not a life we should impose on a child in the name of some greater heritage value. This argument is predicated on the assumption that a cultural heritage is not a mean-ingful set of rituals, values, and metaphors to orient us in life, but our owner, who has the right to lock us up for the sake of its own honor.

The same folks who would never claim that DNA is destiny, claim precisely that in the case of voiceless children. If you are born an "untouchable" in India, does that caste or caste system own you? Are you morally obligated to remain in that culture? We would never tell an adult that he was bound by cultural norms—imagine insisting that a gay Iranian stay in Iran and suffer the consequences in the name of cultural heritage? According to our liberal Western ideals (of which I am very much a part), adults are not expected to sacrifice themselves on the altar of racial, cultural, or sexual identity as defined by society. Why should children?

"Adoption robs countries of their most precious resource."

This assumes that children are the property of the nation, culture, or religion into which they were born (and even that assumes ge-netic purity). We certainly do not make these claims for adults. If an adult wants to leave a country, religion, or culture, would anyone tell them they are obligated to their old ways? "You were born an ultra-Orthodox Jew and you may be a woman who wants to be-come a rabbi but you are obligated to stay in Crown Heights and cover your hair and have ten children—you are Orthodoxy's most precious resource!" Why are children different?

Harvard Law School professor Elizabeth Bartholet challenges us to a thought experiment. Imagine if children could speak for themselves, regardless of their age, and they were asked if they would prefer to live in an institution or on the streets in their country of birth over living with a family outside their country of birth. What does our empathy, our imagination, tell us? If, God forbid, our children were ever orphaned, what would we want for them? And at this point, for millions of children, that IS the choice.

"International adoption is corrupt."

Abuses in international adoption certainly do exist, but shutting down international adoption is a cruel response. In "The Debate" in *Intercountry Adoption: Policies, Practices, and Outcomes* (Ashgate Publishing, 2012), Professor Bartholet writes

> that this makes no sense as a way of addressing adoption law violations. It punishes unparented children by locking them into institutions and denying them the nurturing adoptive homes they need. It puts children at far greater risk of true trafficking and exploitation . . . The response to adoption abuses should be the same as in other areas of law violation—enforce existing law, strengthen that law as appropriate, and punish those violating the law . . . Some say that it is hard for poor countries with limited infrastructure to enforce laws prohibiting baby selling and other adoption abuses. This may be. But it is also hard, indeed impossible, for these countries to guarantee nurturing parental homes for all their children. Even if adoption law violations occur, the harm such violations cause children and birth parents is minimal compared to the harm caused by shutting down or severely restricting international adoption.

The chocolate we eat (unless it's fair or direct trade) is often the product of child slavery in cocoa production. In Ghana the fishing industry is "manned" ("childed"?) by small children whose fingers are thin enough to work the fine underwater netting. These kids are bought, stolen, and tricked away from their parents into forced labor, often death (have you ever gotten caught in an underwater net?). Yet no one demands to stop all chocolate production. No one is erasing fish from the menu at their favorite restaurant in Ghana or anywhere. It seems that, to many, leaving millions of children without parents is a reasonable trade for stopping abuses in an adoption system, but giving up chocolate? Well, that's asking too much.

"Nations are pressured—as Romania was in order to join the EU—to make the orphan crisis 'disappear.'"

On a micro-scale we would never condone hiding child abuse to save face. But on a macro-scale very few people care.

"Why spend $28,000 on the adoption of one child when that money could support many more people?"

The money comes from adoptive parents for the purpose of adopting a child who would otherwise have no family, not from funds that support communities. We do not have to choose between resources for sustainability and resources for adoption.

"Adoption is merely colonialism wrapped in a humanistic package."

I wish we lived in a world in which no one group dominates or colonizes another—or ever has. Prohibiting, or slowing down, international adoption does not increase egalitarianism in the world.

The biblical flood story describes the generation of Noah as so evil that God decided to destroy the world and start humanity over again. There is a rabbinic story that says that the waters did not fall as rain but instead came up from the earth like geysers. What did the generation of Noah do? They took their babies and stuffed them into the holes to plug the water flow and save themselves. That is this anti-international-adoption reality: using our children to stop the flows of injustice we adults have created. Any sane person agrees that social ills must be addressed. But we don't use children to do that. Especially since using children as tools only increases the exact kind of suffering we want to end.

Acknowledgments

So many people helped make this story happen—in life and into this book. My parents' immense love shepherded me my whole life. Just months before publication, my mother died after a long illness—through most of which she continued directing plays and giving generously to everyone who crossed her path, mostly me. Her wisdom sustained me. Her husband, John, pre-deceased her, but his steady, fatherly love still held us all. My remaining parents are the crazy ones, and I would have it no other way. Donald and Janice Silverman are rocks for their children and grandchildren, and I love you like crazy. I am so blessed to have had four parents to love me. And an aunt, Martha Pleasure—I love you and am so grateful for you and my cousins. You and Mom taught my sisters and me how to be the kind of siblings we are. And my sisters, Laura, Jodyne, and Sarah—near or far—were always at my side and had my back. I love you like crazy cakes. YM4E. And to my hearts: Aliza, Hallel, Adar, Zamir, and Ashira. Thank you for letting me write the whole story, the not-so-flattering parts, too. And thank you for becoming the breathtakingly beautiful forces that you are. I love you the whole earth and the whole sky. To Pat Delzell, who was by Mom's—and our—sides our whole life. We love you. And to the women who lovingly cared for my boys until they came home. You gave gifts for which you can never be repaid. I strive to be like you. Thank you to Sam Seder and to Lara Kislinger for your loving, adventurous spirits. Thanks to my honorary family Leah Schraga, Mali Mantasnot, Ziva Birasau, Shira Greenberg, Yonit Tefate, and Lital Polanski for lovingly keeping our family functioning despite all odds. And to Esther Ben Gigi for saving us. Loving friends at my side, with red pens in hand, include Leslie Lawrence, Rabbi Susan Fendrick, Rabbi Sharon Cohen Anisfeld, Rabbi Susan Harris, Rabbi Dianne Cohler-Esses, Rabbi Sarra Lev, Rachel Kadish, Sara Cohen, Lisa Coll, and my awesome mother-in-law, Devora Abramowitz. To Rebbitz Yisrael Campbell, thank you for distracting me from writing every day, and Paula Weiman-Kelman for the beautiful video of Adar's homecoming. And, for her wisdom, skill, love, and saintly patience, Judy Bolton Fasman. Jami Bernard of Barncat Publishing is a genius, and this book would not exist without her. If you are a writer, hire her. Tovah Lazaroff helped a very little bit, I think. Maybe she was there from the beginning and moved me forward, in baby steps, toward the vision that became this book, and I could not have written it without her. I don't really remember, but I love her anyway. Thanks to Paul Beatty for being Paul, to Charlie Kalech and J-Towne Internet Services for developing JustAdopt.net, and Bain Consulting for donating their wisdom. Thank you to the Mandel Foundation for its support, and, with all my heart, to Kibbutz Ketura for the peace, friendship, mountains, and coffee. Thank you to Both Ends Burning and to Elizabeth Bartholet for the tireless work you do on behalf of the most vulnerable, trafficked, and abused humans in the world—unparented children. Anne Hawkins believed in this book in its earliest stages and helped me believe in it, too. Andrew Blauner's enthusiasm and faith carried the book, and me, all the way into the arms of the fabulous, amazing Da Capo Press team: Renee Sedliar, who edited with heart, wisdom, depth, and humor; Carolyn Sobczak and Lisa Zales, who copyedited with brilliant clarity; and Lissa Warren, who imagined its potential impact everywhere. Jonathan Sainsbury's art captured my book perfectly. I am so lucky to benefit from Kevin Hanover's marketing vision. And John Radziewicz made this possible. I am grateful beyond words to be in the Da Capo family. And, above all, to Yosef, for making my life an adventure worth writing about. Love, big time.